Phase Theory and Its Consequences:
The Initial and Recursive Symbol *S*

Phase Theory and Its Consequences:
The Initial and Recursive Symbol S

Edited by
Miyoko Yasui
Manabu Mizuguchi

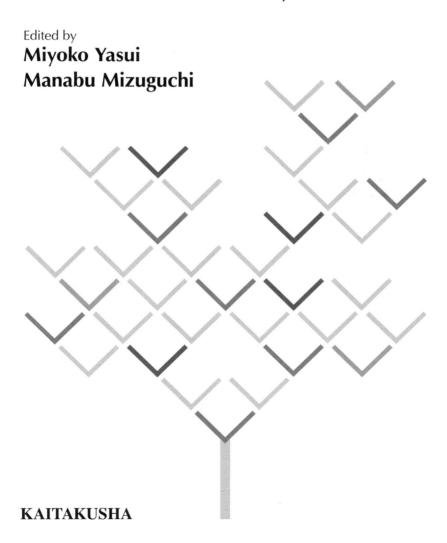

KAITAKUSHA

Kaitakusha Co., Ltd.
5-2, Mukogaoka 1-chome
Bunkyo-ku, Tokyo 113-0023
Japan

Phase Theory and Its Consequences:
The Initial and Recursive Symbol S

Published in Japan
by Kaitakusha Co., Ltd., Tokyo

Copyright © 2016
by Miyoko Yasui et al.

All rights reserved. No part of this publication may be reproduced, stored in a retrieval system, or transmitted, in any form or by any means, electronic, mechanical, photocopying, recording, or otherwise, without the prior permission of the copyright owner.

First published 2016

Printed and bound in Japan
by ARM Corporation

Cover design by Shihoko Nakamura

Table of Contents

Introduction: The Initial and Recursive Symbol *S*
....*Miyoko Yasui*   1

Contextual Phasehood and the Ban on Extraction from Complements of Lexical Heads: When Does X Become a Phase?
....*Željko Bošković*   5

Simplest Merge, Labeling, and A′-Movement of the Subject
....*Manabu Mizuguchi*   41

Labeling Ambiguity in the Root Context and Sentence-Final Particles
....*Miyoko Yasui and Yoshiro Asayama*   85

Island Repair and the Derivation by Phase
....*Hidekazu Tanaka*   119

Verbal Affix Deletion in Indonesian Quotative Inversion
....*Kazuhide Chonan*   151

List of Contributors

Yoshiro Asayama
Department of Interdisciplinary Studies
Dokkyo University, Japan
yasayama01@dokkyo.ac.jp

Manabu Mizuguchi
Department of Social Psychology
Toyo University, Japan
mizuguchi@toyo.jp

Željko Bošković
Department of Linguistics
University of Connecticut, USA
zeljko.boskovic@uconn.edu

Hidekazu Tanaka
Faculty of Letters
Okayama University, Japan
hidekazu@okayama-u.ac.jp

Kazuhide Chonan
Department of Japanese Letters
Universitas Darma Persada, Indonesia
indojaman@ae.auone-net.jp

Miyoko Yasui
Department of English
Dokkyo University, Japan
myasui@dokkyo.ac.jp

Introduction: The Initial and Recursive Symbol *S*

Miyoko Yasui

The book contains a selection of papers from two workshops, one held at Dokkyo University titled "Phase and Merge" on November 7, 2014 and the other at the annual meeting of the English Linguistic Society of Japan titled "On the Phasehood of CP and Other Projections" on November 8, 2014. The focus of the workshops is to shed some light into the architecture of undoubtedly the most fundamental unit of any natural language, which has been given the symbol S in earlier generative research. The symbol S has been given a significant status in two respects. Specifically in the *Aspects* model, (i) "S is the designated initial symbol of the grammar," which initiates successive applications of rewriting rules to derive deep phrase structures, and (ii) the phrase structure rules "may introduce the initial symbol S into a line of derivation," from which "[t]he infinite generative capacity of the grammar arises" (Chomsky 1965:75, 142). In other words, "the recursive property is a feature of the base component, in particular, of the rules that introduce the initial symbol S in designated positions in strings of category symbols" (Chomsky 1965:137). A question arises if S as the initial symbol is completely on a par with S that can be introduced as an embedded clause.

In *Aspects*, root and embedded clauses are distinguished as #S# and S', respectively, where "# is the boundary symbol" that marks the edges of the whole sentence. The details of S' are not clear, but it "is a variant of the sentence" and unlike in later theories, it does not include a complementizer (Chomsky 1965:75, 92–94). The distinction has received much empirical support and remained one of the theoretically significant issues in current syntactic theories. In particular, the subject-auxiliary inversion is canonically restricted to matrix questions in English and other languages with similar operations. Other types of inversion in English such as locative and quotative inversion are observed only in the root context. Japanese and many other languages have so-called sentence-final particles that cannot attach to embedded clauses. Right dislocation in many languages is possible only in the root context. These are main data covered in this collection of papers.

S in the *Aspects* model is exocentric, as mentioned recently by Chomsky (2013:43), who further says that it is "clearly preferable to the X-bar theoretic stipulations" and assumes that "structures need not be endocentric." As for the locus of tense and other functional features essential for clauses, the *Aspects* model assumes the following, where details such as concatenation symbols and other phrase structure rules are omitted:

(1) a. S → NP Predicate-Phrase
 b. Predicate-Phrase → Aux VP (Place) (Time)
 c. VP → V $\left\{ \begin{array}{l} \text{(NP) (PP) (PP) (Mariner)} \\ \text{S}' \end{array} \right\}$
 d. Aux → Tense (M) (Aspect)
 (Chomsky 1965:105)

According to (1a–d), tense is the obligatory constituent of Aux, which in turn is introduced into syntactic structure obligatorily with VP. Going further back to Chomsky's (1957:39) framework, tense and other clausal features are obligatory elements of Aux, but they form a constituent with the main verb (Verb in (2b, c)).

(2) a. Sentence → NP VP
 b. VP → Verb + NP
 c. Verb → Aux + V
 d. Aux → C (M) (have + en) (be + ing)

Various proposals have been advanced under the assumption that clauses are endocentric. For example, Jackendoff (1977) and Marantz (1980) claim that S is the maximal projection of V. In the seventies, S′ is assumed to consist of C(omp) and S, which can be restated as CP being a projection of S. It follows from this short historical review that C, T, and V are related structurally, if not projectionally. An important question to be raised here is which of the three intrinsically possesses tense and other clausal features. Chomsky (2008) and Richards (2007), *inter alia*, assume that they originate in C and are handed downward to T/V, while Grimshaw (1997), Broekhuis (2013), den Dikken 2006), Gallego and Uriagereka (2006) take the opposite view: the features are extended upward from the T/V domain to C. The headedness/labeling of clauses and the downward versus upward sharing of clausal features are key theoretical issues in this book.

This book contains five papers from the afore-mentioned two workshops, all of which have been dedicated to the elucidation of clausal structures based on the accomplishments accumulated in generative grammar. The issue shared by the first three papers is on labeling of the initial and recursive symbols as well as other syntactic objects. Željko Bošković observes that in a configuration where a phasal head takes a phase as its complement, extraction is banned from the complement of the lower phase. An account of the ban is proposed where XP functions as a phase only after it is merged into the structure, with movement to the edge of XP driven by the need to undergo successive-cyclic movement without violating the Phase-Impenetrability Condition taking place after this merger.

Manabu Mizuguchi explores the syntax of subject A′-movement under simplest Merge. It is claimed that a subject *wh*-phrase (more generally, a subject operator) is internally merged only as Spec,CP, moving vacuously to Spec,TP, which is argued to be a Minimalist version of the Vacuous Movement Hypothesis. A-properties of the subject directly merged in Spec,CP follow from head movement, which is argued to be feature climbing from lower to higher heads. It is also demonstrated that lack of EPP effects on T as well as ECP or *that*-trace effects can be deduced from simple computation (i.e., simplest Merge) and its interactions with the interface systems.

Miyoko Yasui and Yoshiro Asayama demonstrate that Japanese and other East-Asian languages, which lack overt agreement phenomena, have S-final particles that can be used S-internally with a variety of categories other than finite predicates. If labeling of a syntactic object formed of non-heads by free Merge must resort to movement of one of the non-heads and feature agreement in its landing site, the same operations should not be available in languages without feature agreement. It is argued that the distributional versatility of the S-final particles is a kind of labeling ambiguity, which is resolved due to their unrestricted selectional properties. It is speculated that the S-final particles function to terminate the computation properly without recourse to feature agreement.

The remaining two papers deal with the so-called root phenomena observed in the domain of the initial symbol: right-dislocation and quotative inversion. Hidekazu Tanaka argues that island repair is not a general property of ellipsis: Some elliptical constructions such as sluicing cancel island violations, while others such as right-dislocation in Japanese do not. Adopting LF-copying account of island repair (Chung, Ladusaw, and McCloskey 1995), it is demonstrated that those constructions that do not permit island repair cannot be interpreted through LF-copying, which forces PF-deletion, and consequently, can result in island violations.

Kazuhide Chonan discusses one of the interesting phenomena in

Indonesian syntax: verbal affix deletion. *MeN-* and *ber-*, which are prefixed to transitive and unergative roots, are deleted in seemingly unrelated constructions: zero-passives, within relative clauses, imperatives, and quotative inversion. Focusing on the last construction, Chonan compares its syntactic and information structures in English and Indonesian, and concludes that Quote, the verb, and the subject are positioned higher in Indonesian than in English. The generalization deduced from the analyses of quotative and other constructions is that a verbal root cannot bear more than one V-related feature in Indonesian, unlike the finite copular and aspectual verbs in English, which are assumed to move from V to C via T in matrix questions.

The publication of this book has been subsidized by Dokkyo University Grant for Academic Publications.

References

Broekhuis, Hans. 2013. Feature inheritance versus extended projections. Ms. Meertens Institute, Amsterdam.
Chomsky, Noam. 1957. *Syntactic structures*. The Hague: Mouton de Gruyter.
Chomsky, Noam. 1965. *Aspects of the theory of syntax*. Cambridge, MA: MIT Press.
Chomsky, Noam. 2008. On phases. In *Foundational issues in linguistic theory: Essays in honor of Jean-Roger Vergnaud*, eds. by Robert Freidin, Carlos P. Otero, and Maria Luisa Zubizarreta, 133–166. Cambridge, MA: MIT Press.
Chomsky, Noam. 2013. Problems of projection. *Lingua* 130:33–49.
Chung, Sandra, William A. Ladusaw, and James McCloskey. 1995. Sluicing and logical form. *Natural Language Semantics* 3:239–282.
Dikken, Marcel den. 2006. *Relators and linkers: The syntax of predication, predicate inversion, and copulas*. Cambridge, MA: MIT Press.
Gallego, Ángel and Juan Uriagereka. 2006. Sub-extraction from subjects. Paper presented at West Coast Conference on Formal Linguistics (WCCFL) 25 and Linguistic Symposium on Romance Languages (LSRL) 36, 1 April.
Grimshaw, Jane. 1997. Projection, heads and optimality. *Linguistic Inquiry* 28:373–422.
Jackendoff, Ray. 1977. *X' syntax: A study of phrase structure*. Cambridge, MA: MIT Press.
Marantz, Alec. 1981. On the nature of grammatical relations. Doctoral dissertation, MIT, Cambridge, MA.
Richards, Marc D. 2007. On feature inheritance: an argument from the Phase Impenetrability Condition. *Linguistic Inquiry* 38:563–572.

Contextual Phasehood and the Ban on Extraction from Complements of Lexical Heads: When Does X Become a Phase?*

Željko Bošković

In a double-phase configuration, where a phasal head takes a phase as its complement, extraction is banned from the complement of the lower phase. An account of the ban is proposed where XP functions as a phase only after it is merged into the structure, with movement to the edge of XP driven by the need to undergo successive-cyclic movement without violating the Phase-Impenetrability Condition taking place after this merger.

Keywords: islands, phases, spell-out, successive-cyclic movement, the Phase-Impenetrability Condition

1 Introduction

Ross (1967) established the constraint in (1), where complex NP is a noun modified by a clause.[1]

(1) The Complex NP Constraint (CNPC): Extraction from complex NPs is disallowed.

The effect of (1) is illustrated by (2).

(2) *How$_i$ did you hear [$_{NP}$ rumors [$_{CP}$ that [$_{IP}$ John bought a house t$_i$]]]?

Extraction is allowed from complex VPs: there is no such thing as Complex VP Constraint, in contrast to the Complex NP Constraint.

(3) How$_i$ did you [$_{VP}$ think [$_{CP}$ that [$_{IP}$ a dog bit John t$_i$]]]?

Previous research on the locality of movement has focused on (3), putting

---

* The paper is based upon work supported by the NSF under Grant BCS-0920888.

[1] I will ignore relative clauses. Since they are adjuncts extraction out of them involves a violation of the traditional Adjunct Condition, that is, the ban on extraction out of adjuncts. (It should be noted here that Safir 1985 shows that (1) cannot be reduced to the Adjunct Condition by treating nominal clausal complements as adjuncts.)

(2) aside. Thus, the works on the locality of movement within minimalism generally ignore (2), the analyses of successive-cyclic movement being developed on the basis of (3). Bošković (2015a), however, argues that that move has been fundamentally misguided since (2) represents a pervasive pattern found in many contexts, (3) being highly exceptional. In particular, (with some exceptions to be discussed below) extraction is banned not only from clausal, but all complements of nouns. Furthermore, APs, PPs, and ergative VPs pattern with NPs: extraction is also banned from the complement of adjectives, prepositions, and ergative verbs.[2] The only exception to the general ban on extraction out of complements of lexical heads (the Complex XP Constraint) in fact concerns transitive, non-ergative VP. Since this case has been used to build theories of successive-cyclic movement, the existing theories of successive-cyclic movement make such movement too easy. This paper proposes a new account of the ban on extraction from complements of lexical heads (also sharpening the exact formulation of the ban in question by restating it in more general phase-theoretic terms), which makes successive-cyclic movement in general more difficult while still leaving room to allow it in (3).

The analysis proposed in the paper is crucially based on a contextual approach to phasehood, where XP functions as a phase only after it is merged into the structure. As a result, movement to the edge of XP driven by the need to undergo successive-cyclic movement without violating the Phase-Impenetrability Condition (PIC) takes place after this merger, which will be shown to deduce the ban on extraction from complements of lexical heads.[3] What will be crucial in the deduction is that under the approach to phases argued for here, all the examples that motivate the ban in question involve a configuration where a phasal head takes a phase as its complement, a configuration which will be shown to be very recalcitrant to extraction.

I will start the discussion by generalizing the CNPC, then turn to the deduction of the generalized CNPC, also exploring some consequences of the proposed deduction.

---

[2] The same actually holds for passive verbs, which will not be discussed here.
[3] See Bošković (2015a) for an alternative account of the locality effect in question based on Chomsky's (2013) labeling system and antilocality, and Bošković (2015b) for an alternative account based on phasal spell-out (i.e., on the assumption that what is sent to spell-out is the phase itself, as in the original phase theory).

2 On the Complex XP Constraint[4]

The CNPC concerns clausal complements. However, extraction is banned not only from clausal complements of nouns, but all complements of nouns. This is illustrated by the contrast between (4) and (5) and the contrast between (6) and (7) (such contrasts were originally noted in Bach and Horn 1976 and Chomsky 1973).[5]

(4) Of who(m)$_i$ did you see [friends t$_i$]?
(5)??Of who(m)$_i$ did you see [$_{NP}$ enemies of friends t$_i$]?
(6) Who$_i$ did you see [friends of t$_i$]?
(7)?*Who did you see [$_{NP}$ enemies of friends of t$_i$]?

Note that I assume a reanalysis/pruning account of P-stranding, where there is no PP in (6) (see, e.g., Stepanov 2012), which means that, like (4), (6) involves extraction of a nominal complement, in contrast to (7), which involves extraction out of a nominal complement. (In section 3.3, I will however give an account of P-stranding where there is a PP in (6). Pending section 3.3, I will put P-stranding aside; at any rate, the relevant contrast holds even without P-stranding, as in (4) and (5) and other data discussed below.)

Consider in this respect Greek. In Greek, both genitive DPs and PPs function as nominal complements. Both cases exhibit a simple/deep extraction contrast, as illustrated in (8)–(11), extraction being disallowed from the complement of a noun.

---

[4] This section and section 5 sum up some of the relevant arguments from Bošković (2015a); the reader is referred to that work for additional arguments and discussion (the data where the source is not noted come from that work, except for (11b), which is due to C. Christopoulos and M. Stavrou (p.c.)). Note also that since weak islands are sometimes completely weakened with argument extraction (especially with DP argument extraction, see Cinque 1990), adjunct extraction is a more reliable diagnostic, hence adjunct extraction will be used whenever possible. However, in English it can be tested only with clausal complements, adjunct extraction quite generally being disallowed from DPs in English, as in *From which city$_i$ did Peter meet [girls t$_i$] (see Chomsky 1986). (Another interfering factor that arises with argument but not with adjunct extraction, which makes the latter more reliable, concerns phase collapsing from section 4 (and more generally reanalysis), an effect found with argument but not adjunct extraction, see Bošković (2015a) for relevant discussion in this respect.)

[5] We are dealing here with argument extraction (see footnote 4), hence the locality violations are weaker. Note that for ease of exposition, I will only mark the relevant NP in the unacceptable examples.

(8) Tu   vivliu$_i$ mu ipes   pos dhiavases tin [kritiki t$_i$]
    the-GEN   book-GEN me said-2S that read-2S   the review
    'You told me you read the review of the book.'
    (Horrocks and Stavrou 1987)

(9) *Tu   vivliu$_i$ mu ipes   pos dhiavases tin [$_{NP}$ enstasi
    the-GEN   book-GEN me said-2S that read-2S   the   objection
    [tis   kritikis t$_i$]]
    the-GEN review-GEN
    'You told me you read the objection to the review of the book.'

(10) Se t$_i$;   eksefrasan   ton [antilogo t$_i$]?
     to   what   expressed-3P the objection
     'To what did they express the objection?'

(11) a. *Se t$_i$;   eksefrasan   [$_{NP}$ epikrisi [tu   antilogu t$_i$]]?
        to   what   expressed-3P   criticism the-GEN objection-GEN
        'To what did they express criticism of the objection?'
     b. *Tis   kritikis$_i$ eksefrasan   ton [$_{NP}$ antilogo [se
        the-GEN review-GEN expressed-3P the   objection to
        epikrisi t$_i$]]?
        criticism
        'They expressed the objection to criticism of the review.'

These examples indicate that extraction from the complement of a noun is quite generally disallowed. There is nothing special about CPs in this respect: extraction from a nominal complement is disallowed regardless of the categorial status of the complement. (1) should then be generalized as in (12) (the Generalized Complex NP Constraint).

(12) Extraction out of nominal complements is disallowed.

The generalized version of the CNPC holds for other lexical heads as well. Consider first adjectives, starting with the CNPC context. Extraction from APs headed by adjectives modified by clauses is disallowed, on a par with complex NPs. Thus, (13) is unacceptable if the adjuncts modify the embedded clause.

(13) *How$_i$/Why$_i$ are you [$_{AP}$ proud [$_{CP}$ that John hired Mary t$_i$]]?

As in the case of nouns, the effect is not confined to clausal complements of adjectives: extraction is also banned from non-CP complements of adjectives, as illustrated by (14).

(14) a. Of who(m)$_i$ is he [proud t$_i$]?
b.?*Of who(m)$_i$ is he [$_{AP}$ proud of [friends t$_i$]]?

Recall that nouns can take either genitive DP or PP complements in Greek, extraction being disallowed out of both DP and PP complements of nouns. Greek adjectives can also take either genitive DPs or PPs as their complements. In both cases, extraction from the complement of *responsible* is banned.

(15) *Tu   ktiriu$_i$ [$_{AP}$ ipefthinos   [tu   fotismu t$_i$]]
     the-GEN building-GEN   is-responsible   the-GEN lighting-GEN
     'the building he is responsible for the lighting of'

(16) *Tu   ktiriu$_i$ [$_{AP}$ ipefthinos   [gia to   fotismo t$_i$]]
     the-GEN building-GEN   is-responsible   for the lighting
     'the building he is responsible for the lighting of'

APs thus pattern with NPs regarding extraction from their complements. In addition to (12), we then also have the Generalized Complex AP Constraint in (17).

(17) Extraction out of adjectival complements is disallowed.

Furthermore, PPs pattern with NPs and APs in the relevant respect. (18) replicates the simple/deep extraction contrast from NPs/APs that was discussed above (see also Landau 2009).

(18) a. Who$_i$ did you read [about t$_i$]?
b.?*Of who(m)$_i$ did you read [$_{PP}$ about [friends t$_i$]]?

Consider now the CNPC context with PPs. Prepositions can take finite CP complements in Spanish. Significantly, extraction is disallowed out of such complements.[6]

(19) a. *¿cómo$_i$ se   acordó   [$_{PP}$ de [$_{CP}$ que [Pedro
        how   clitic   (s)he.remembered   of   that   Pedro
        preparaba   la   comida t$_i$]]]
        prepared.imperfect   the   food
    cf. b. se acordó de que Pedro preparaba la comida.

---

[6] Some languages treat (some) prepositions as inherent Case-markers, see in this respect Nunes (2009). Such prepositions are not relevant to our concerns (the discussion here concerns lexical categories).

That extraction from complements of prepositions is banned is confirmed by Greek (20).[7]

(20) *Tinos$_i$ endhiaferese   [$_{PP}$ ya [ti fili t$_i$]]
     who-GEN be-interested-2S   for the friend
     'Whose friend are you interested in?'
     (Horrocks and Stavrou 1987)

The above data provide evidence for the existence of the Generalized Complex PP Constraint (21).

(21) Extraction out of complements of prepositions is disallowed.

Why are then VPs different when it comes to extraction from their complements? Before providing an answer to the question it is important to note that they are not always different. The locality effect in question is actually found with ergative VPs. Thus, (22), involving a non-ergative context, is better than (23), which involves an ergative verb.

(22) Who did they [see [(some) friends of t$_i$]] yesterday?

(23)?*Who$_i$ did there [arrive [(some) friends of t$_i$]] last week?

Only argument extraction, which yields a weaker effect than adjunct extraction, can be checked with English DPs (see footnote 4). Belletti and Rizzi (1988), however, show that some psych verbs which take CP arguments are ergative (see sections 5-6 for ergatives with just a CP argument). (24)-(26) involve uncontroversially ergative psych verbs, where the CP is standardly assumed to be located in the V-complement position (see, e.g., Belletti and Rizzi 1988, Pesetsky 1995, Landau 2009). Both argument and adjunct extraction are degraded in this context, the latter being worse, as expected.[8]

(24) a.??What$_i$ did it appeal to Mary [that John fixed t$_i$]?
     b. *How$_i$ did it appeal to Mary [that John fixed the car t$_i$]?

(25) a.??What$_i$ did it depress Mary [that John sold t$_i$]?
     b. *How$_i$ did it depress Mary [that John was fired t$_i$]?

---

[7] (11b) and (16) are actually also relevant here.

[8] (24)-(26) may involve short V-movement, which may exist in English even independently of v (i.e., V-to-v), see in this respect Johnson (1991) and Lasnik (1999).

(26) a. ??What$_i$ does it bother Bill [that John underestimates t$_i$]?
    b. *How$_i$ does it bother Bill [that John fixed the car t$_i$]?

There are also transitive ergatives that do not take CP arguments. Only argument extraction can be checked in such cases. Importantly, extraction is degraded in this context (see also Belletti and Rizzi 1988 for the same observation regarding Italian).

(27) ??Who$_i$ did your behavior bother [the sister of t$_i$]]?
    (Johnson 1992)

(28) ?*Who$_i$ did John's embarrassment escape [friends of t$_i$]]?

The Generalized Complex VP Constraint effects thus emerge with ergative verbs: ergative verbs pattern with nouns, adjectives, and prepositions in the relevant respect.

(29)   Extraction out of complements of ergative verbs is disallowed.

When properly generalized, the CNPC thus represents a pervasive pattern found in many contexts. Extraction is banned not only from clausal but all nominal complements. Furthermore, APs, PPs, and ergative VPs pattern with NPs: extraction is banned from their complements regardless of the categorial status of the complement.[9] With the exception of non-ergative verbs, extraction is then banned from all complements of all lexical heads. In other words, (1) should be generalized as in (30).

(30)   **The Complex XP Constraint** (where X ≠ non-ergative V)
    Extraction out of complements of lexical heads is disallowed.

3 Deducing the Complex XP Constraint

3.1 The Theory of Phases

I now turn to the deduction of (30). I will first restate (30) within the phase theory of Bošković (2015a) and then propose a new deduction of (30), different from the one proposed in Bošković (2015a) (as well as Bošković 2015b).

Chomsky (2000) proposes a context-independent approach to phasehood where certain phrases (vP and CP) are always phases regardless of

---

[9] See also Bošković (2015a) on passives; it is noted in that work that the locality effect in question is also found with passive verbs.

their syntactic context. A number of authors have, however, argued that the phase status of X can be affected by its syntactic context. Thus, based on a number of arguments regarding the locality of movement and the distribution of ellipsis, Bošković (2012, 2013a, 2014) argues that the highest projection in the extended domain of a lexical head/clause functions as a phase. In this system, vP is a phase as the highest projection in the extended domain of V and CP is a phase as the highest clausal projection. There is a phase even with ergatives even if vP, which is responsible for external θ-role assignment, is absent with ergatives; in that case VP is a phase as the highest projection in the domain of V.

Another way to look at this is from the perspective of Grohmann (2003), where a clause is divided into three domains, the discourse, the agreement, and the θ-domain, and movement must pass through each domain. Suppose that, as proposed in Bošković (2015a), we collapse the agreement and the discourse domain into one domain, giving us two domains: thematic and non-thematic. This in fact corresponds to Chomsky's original conception of phases if we assume that the highest projection in a domain functions as a phase. vP is then a phase as the highest projection in the thematic domain, and CP is a phase as the highest projection in the non-thematic domain. With ergatives, due to the lack of vP, VP is the highest projection in the thematic domain hence a phase. (The presence of a non-θ-marking vP with ergatives would not affect anything (hence this possibility will be ignored below): VP would still be a phase.)[10] I will adopt here this approach to phases: the highest projection in the thematic domain of every lexical head and the highest projection in the non-thematic/functional domain function as phases.

Significantly, under this approach to phases all the examples that instantiate (30) which were discussed above involve the context in (31), where a phasal head takes a phase as its complement.

(31) [$_{XP=Phase}$ [$_{YP=Phase}$]]

To illustrate, NP is a phase in (2) as the highest projection in the nominal thematic domain. The same holds for AP in (13) and PP in (19), as the highest projections in the A/P thematic domains. Focusing on the NP case,

---

[10] This is an important diffence from Bošković (2013a, 2014), where the thematic domain does not form a separate phasal domain, hence ergative VP is not a phase unless it is the only projection in the extended domain of V.

the noun takes CP, which is a phase, as its complement in (2), hence (2) involves a double-phase context from (31). The same holds for Greek (9), which involves a DP phase right below the NP phase. All the unacceptable extractions from nominal complements discussed above in fact involve (31). The same holds for the examples involving the AP constraint from (17): all the unacceptable extractions from the complement of an adjective involve the context in (31). Thus, the adjective, a phase head, takes a CP phase complement in (13) and a DP/PP phase complement in Greek (15)–(16). The same holds for prepositions: preposition, a phasal head, also takes a phase as its complement in all the cases of (21), given in (18)–(20).

Consider also the VP cases, that is, examples (22)–(28). Recall that ergatives behave differently from other verbs in that they show Complex XP Constraint effects. Given the difference, the obvious conclusion is that vP is what matters here. With non-ergative verbs, vP is the highest projection in the verbal thematic domain. VP is then not a phase. As a result, extraction from clausal complements of non-ergative verbs, as in (32), does not involve the context in (31). In contrast, ergatives lack the thematic vP layer. This means that VP is the highest (and only) projection in the relevant thematic domain hence a phase in (33). (33) then involves a double-phase configuration, that is, the context from (31).[11]

(32) How$_i$ did you [$_{vP}$ [$_{VP}$ think [$_{CP}$ that [$_{IP}$ John fixed the car t$_i$]]]]?

(33) *How$_i$ did it [$_{VP}$ appeal to Mary [$_{CP}$ that [$_{IP}$ John fixed the car t$_i$]]]?

Extraction is thus disallowed in the configuration in (31), where a phasal head takes a phase as its complement. We can then restate (30) as in (34). ((34) will be slightly revised below).

(34) The Phase-over-Phase Constraint
Extraction is banned from phases that function as complements of phasal heads (i.e., the double-phase configuration from (31)).

Recall now our initial question: why is it that there is no Complex VP Constraint, in contrast to the Complex NP Constraint as well as the Complex AP Constraint and the Complex PP Constraint. A clue for the answer to the question is provided by the existence of Complex VP Constraint effects with ergatives. The obvious difference between ergative and non-ergative

---

[11] Phases are given in boldface. For ease of exposition, I ignore V-movement here since it does not affect anything.

verbs is the existence of vP with the latter. (34) capitalizes on this: the current approach to phases yields a principled difference (which will be deduced below) between ergative and non-ergative verbs given the presence of (θ-assigning) vP with the latter. Generalizing this, the reason for the different behavior of non-ergative VP and NP/AP/PP/ergative VP regarding the Complex XP Constraint is the presence of vP, that is, the assignment of the external θ-role in a projection distinct from VP. There is then no such projection with NP/AP/PP. nP/pP/aP are sometimes posited merely for the sake of uniformity with VP. But the fact is that there is actually no uniformity here when it comes to extraction.[12]

I now turn to a deduction of (34), a restatement of (30) made possible by the approach to phases where the highest projection in thematic/non-thematic domains functions as a phase.

3.2 Deducing the Complex XP Constraint: Only Phrases Can Be Phases
As discussed above, all the examples that instantiate (30) involve the context from (31), repeated here as (35), a configuration where a phasal head takes a phase as its complement (e.g., [$_{NP}$ [$_{CP}$ in (2); [$_{NP}$ [$_{DP}$ in (9); [$_{VP}$ [$_{CP}$ in (24)). In light of this, (30) can be restated as in (34), repeated here as (36).

(35) [$_{XP=Phase}$ [$_{YP=Phase}$]]

(36) The Phase-over-Phase Constraint
Extraction is banned from phases that function as complements of phasal heads (i.e. the double-phase configuration from (35)).

We are now ready to turn to the deduction of the locality effect in question. In what follows, I will adopt the phase-based approach to the cycle, where cyclicity is defined on phases. In this approach to the cycle, movement need not target the top of the structure as long as it does not return to lower phasal domains. The standard assumption that spell-out proceeds cyclically, with complements of phasal heads being sent to spell-out, in fact imposes natural cyclicity: when something is spelled out its cycle is "left behind," hence nothing can be moved within it or from it.

In a contextual phasehood approach, and the approach to phasehood argued for here is contextual, (at least in some cases) whether XP is a phase or not can be determined only after it is embedded into larger syntactic

---

[12] It is important to note that n/p/aP could still exist, but they would not be part of the thematic domain (i.e., they would not be assigning a θ-role).

structure, since context determines phasehood. More precisely, the next merger determines the phasehood of XP. To illustrate, given that, as discussed above, the highest projection in the non-thematic/functional domain functions as a phase, if IP is merged with a non-thematic, purely functional head like C, IP will not be a phase, but if IP is merged with a lexical head like N, IP will be a phase (as the highest projection in the non-thematic/functional domain; see section 5 for empirical evidence to this effect).

To capture the next-merger property of phasehood in the contextual phasehood approach, I then adopt (37): in the Bare Phrase Structure system (see Chomsky 1995), X is a phrase if it no longer projects; X is then unambiguously a phrase only if it is merged with Y, with Y projecting.

(37)   X is a phase only if it is an unambiguous X^{max}.

The underlying intuition here is that only phrases can be phases.[13]

I also make the natural assumption that X can be targeted by movement due to the need to undergo successive-cyclic movement without violating the PIC (see Chomsky 2000, 2001), which I will refer to as phasal edgehood, only if X is a phase (see Kang 2014 for evidence to this effect), which, given (37), means only after the first merger of X, that is, after X is embedded in larger structure.

Consider now the derivation of (3) (*How$_i$ did you think [that a dog bit John t$_i$]*) under the above assumptions, starting at the point when the embedded clause is built.

(38) a.   [$_{CP}$ [$_{IP}$ ...... how]]   *How* cannot move to SpecCP since CP is still not a phase.
    b.   V [$_{CP}$ [$_{IP}$ ..... how]]   *How* can now move to SpecCP.
    c.   v [$_{VP}$ [$_{CP}$ how [$_{IP}$]]]   IP is spelled out.

How cannot move to SpecCP at the point when the embedded C is merged into the structure (38a). Since we would be dealing here with movement driven by phasal edgehood, the movement cannot take place until C is merged with another element which then projects; only at that point CP becomes a phase.

After V is merged into the structure, with V projecting, the projection of C becomes a phase hence can be targeted by movement of *how*, driven

---

[13] I assume that (37) always applies, regardless of whether or not a particular instance of phasehood is affected by context.

by phasal edgehood (38b). Given phase-based cyclicity, there is no violation of the cycle here.

Following Chomsky (2001), I assume that insertion of a higher phasal head triggers spell-out of the complement of the lower phasal head.[14] More precisely, as argued in Bošković (2014), I assume that spell-out takes place as soon as the higher phasal head is introduced into the structure. This means that the merger of v in (38c) triggers immediate spell-out of the IP (in other words, it starts a new cycle). Since *how* is outside of the spelled-out unit, it is available for later movement.

Consider now the derivation of (2) (*How_i did you hear rumors [that John bought a house t_i]), an instance of a CNPC violation.

(39) a. [CP [IP ...... how]]   *How* cannot move to SpecCP since CP is still not a phase.
 b. N [CP [IP ..... how]]   IP is spelled out.
 c. N [CP [IP ..... how]]   *How* cannot move since it is contained in a spelled out domain.

As in the case of (3), *how* cannot move to SpecCP right after C is merged into the structure in (2) (step (39a)). However, merger of the next head has a very different effect in (2) than in (3). Since the next head to be merged in (2) is a phasal head, it immediately triggers spell-out of IP (39b). Since *how* is contained within a spelled-out unit, it is then no longer available for movement (39c), hence the ungrammaticality of (2).

Under the analysis presented above, movement to the edge of a phase which is driven by the need to undergo successive-cyclic movement without violating the PIC (i.e., phasal edgehood) is delayed until after the phrase to be targeted by the movement, call it X, is merged (i.e., embedded) into the structure. Since merger of a phasal head triggers immediate spell-out for the lower phase, movement from X is then possible only if X is merged with a non-phasal head (i.e., if the embedding of X involves merger with a non-

---

[14] Note here that, assuming that whether or not an external θ-role is to be assigned is indicated in the θ-grid of the verb (even when it is assigned in SpecvP; see in this respect Sawada 2015), phasal heads in the thematic/lexical domain can be determined locally (phasal heads being N, ergative V, A, P, and v), based on the θ-grid (only a V with an external θ-role does not close the thematic domain with its projection, which means only a V with an external θ-role is not a phasal head). Note, however, that even in these cases, (37) is still relevant in determining a phase (though not a phasal head), see here footnote 13.

phasal head). If X is merged with a phasal head, spell-out will take place before the relevant element, call it Y, moves to the edge of X, as a result of which Y will not be available for movement outside of X.

Wh can then move out of the CP in (40) only in the absence of Y (the bolded elements are phasal heads in (40)).

(40)   **H**   L (**Y**) [$_{CP}$ **C** [$_{IP}$ wh]]

Extraction is thus banned in a phase-over-phase configuration. In other words, we have just deduced the Phase-over-Phase Constraint from (34) and the Generalized XP Constraint from (30) on which (34) was based. We will actually see below that there are some exceptional cases where (30)/(34) do not appear to hold. However, we will also see below that the above deduction of (30)/(34) does leave room to accommodate those exceptional cases; what is important for our purposes right now is that, as the reader can verify, all the ungrammatical cases that have motivated positing (30)/(34) in section 2 can be ruled out by the approach to phases argued for here.

3.3 Phase Complement Movement and P-stranding

We are now in the position to understand why P-stranding does not matter in the contrast between (6)/(4) vs (7)/(5), more precisely, to understand why (6) is grammatical in spite of the Generalized Complex NP Constraint from (12). I will first show that another construction raises a similar issue as (6) and then offer a unified account for that construction and (6).

Recall that, putting aside non-ergative verbs, extraction is not possible from the complement of a lexical head. The complement itself can however move (unless factors independent of those considered here interfere, as in the attempt to move the CP complement of a noun; see Stowell 1981 and Bošković 1995). Thus, while movement from the nominal complement in Greek (9) is not possible, movement of the complement itself, as in (8), is possible.[15]

---

[15] Note that (8) involves movement of a phasal head complement. In fact, a number of examples discussed above involve movement of the complement of a phasal head (e.g., (4), (8), (10), (14a), (18a); in fact the same holds even for simple cases like *John$_i$ arrived t$_i$*). The current discussion then indicates that such movement is in principle possible, contra Abels (2003), who argues that it is not. I will discuss the derivation of examples like (8) directly below. For discussion of Abels's claim in this respect, see Bošković (2015a); I merely note here that the issue with most Abels's examples is that the element that undergoes movement is not a phase itself; such examples are then independently ruled out if only phases can undergo movement, as argued in Chomsky (2000, 2001), Rackowski

Consider then the case where the complement of a noun moves, as in (4), (8), and (10). The relevant configuration is shown abstractly in (41), where K is the complement of N. NP and DP are phases in (41) under the current approach to phases. A number of authors have argued that there is additional structure between NP and DP, hence the presence of XP in (41) (the exact labels and the number of projections in this domain do not matter here, hence I simply use XP).

(41) [$_{DP}$ D [$_{XP}$ X [$_{NP}$ N K]]]

When X is merged into the structure (which activates NP for phasal edge-hood movement), K needs to move to a position where it will be available for movement ouside of the NP phase, that is, it needs to move to the NP edge, given the PIC. K can move to SpecNP. In SpecNP, K is accessible to D, hence it can later move to the DP edge and then outside of the DP.

(42) ... [$_{DP}$ K D [$_{XP}$ X [$_{NP}$ t$_k$ N t$_k$]]]

A number of authors have, however, argued that movement from the complement to the Spec position of the same phrase is not possible (the ban on movement that is too short, often referred to as antilocality; for relevant discussion, see Bošković 1994, 2013a, Saito and Murasugi 1999, Abels 2003, Grohmann 2003, Ticio 2003, Boeckx 2005, among others). If this is indeed the case, the derivation just sketched is not an option (see, however, Chomsky 2015, who crucially argues that such movement is allowed). There is, however, an alternative account which does not require movement from the complement to the Spec of NP. The account allows extraction of the complement of the lower phase in a double-phase configuration; however, it still bans extraction out of the complement. As a result, the account extends to the P-stranding case in (6), which also involves extraction of the lower phase complement in a phase-over-phase configuration.

I will first discuss the account with respect to extraction of the nominal complement, i.e. (41). The account is based on a new conception of the Phase-Impenetrability Condition (PIC), also adopted in the alternative

---

and Richards (2005), Matushansky (2005), Cheng (2012), Harwood (2014), and Bošković (2015c), among others. This is for example the case with (i), where the IP complement of C is not a phase itself. Note in this respect that the problem in question does not arise in the acceptable examples of phasal complement movement noted in this footnote; in all these cases the moved element is a phase.

(i) *[$_{IP}$ Everyone likes Bill]$_i$ John thinks that t$_i$.

analyses of the Complex XP Constraint in Bošković (2015a,b): While for Chomsky (2000, 2001), only the Spec/adjunct of phase KP and its head K are accessible for operations outside of KP, I suggest that Spec/adjunct, head K as well as the complement of K are accessible for operations outside of KP. Nothing within the complement is, however, accessible outside of KP. In other words, I assume the following:

(43) The Phase-Impenetrability Condition
In a phase α with head H, only the immediate domain of H is accessible to operations outside α, where K is in the immediate domain of H if the first node that dominates K is a projection/segment of H.

Since the first node that dominates SpecHP, HP-adjuncts, H-adjuncts, H, and the complement of H is a projection of H, these positions, but nothing else, are accessible to operations outside of HP if HP is a phase. I assume that what is sent to spell-out is the first phrase that is merged with H, that is, the lowest phrase in the immediate domain of H that is not a projection of H (or simply the complement of H).

This conception of the PIC actually fits more naturally with multiple spell-out than Chomsky's and in fact follows Uriagereka's (1999) original conception of multiple spell-out. Uriagereka (see also Nunes and Uriagereka 2000) argues that when a phrase is sent to spell-out, nothing within that phrase is available for further syntactic operations but the phrase itself is available. In Uriagereka's terms, sending X to spell-out, which results in establishing word order within X, turns X essentially into a compound/lexical item whose internal structure is inaccessible to the syntax. X itself is, however, accessible to the syntax. In his conception of the PIC, Chomsky departed from this aspect of Uriagereka's original proposal. The suggestion made here is to return to it.[16]

A side-effect of this approach to the PIC is that it captures Hiraiwa's (2005) claim that what is located at the edge of the edge of phase HP is not at the edge of HP for the purpose of the PIC. Thus, based on a number of cases, Hiraiwa argues that in (44), what is located in SpecXP or adjoined to XP is not located at the edge of HP, that is, it is not accessible to operations

---

[16] Actually, under this conception of the PIC we do not even need the PIC as an independent principle. The assumption that the internal structure of what is sent to spell-out is inaccessible to the syntax is in fact enough.

outside of HP. This in fact follows from (44) since the first node that dominates the positions in question is not a projection of H.

(44)   [$_{HP}$ XP [$_{H'}$ H ...]]

If we put aside (44)/Hiraiwa's claim, as noted in footnote 16, under the current proposal, the PIC (i.e., (43)) is actually not needed as an independent principle in the syntax. The assumption that the internal structure of what is sent to spell-out is inaccessible to the syntax is in fact enough, there is no need to adopt any other assumptions regarding accessibility domains within syntax beyond that. While in what follows I will still use the term PIC for ease of exposition, the reader should bear this in mind.

Returning to the configuration in (41), under (43) D can attract K in (41) even after the complement of N is sent to spell-out. In other words, under Uriagereka's original conception of spell-out (and dispensing with the PIC in the syntax), while nothing within K, which is sent to spell-out, is accessible to D, K itself is accessible to D. As a result, there is no need for K to move to SpecNP prior to moving to the edge of DP (such movement can then be assumed to be banned by antilocality). I emphasize here that while under the above approach to the PIC/spell-out, K is accessible to D, nothing within K is accessible to D. As a result, nothing changes in the previous discussion of the cases that have motivated positing (34).

The analysis also extends to the P-stranding case, without needing to make a recourse to a reanalysis/pruning-style operation for P-stranding (see Bošković 2015a for discussion of that operation). Consider the structure of (6) in (45).

(45)   Who$_i$ did you see [$_{DP}$ t$_i$ [$_{XP}$ [$_{NP}$ t$_i$ friends [$_{PP}$ of   t$_i$]]]]?

Merger of N triggers the spell-out of the complement of the preposition (PP being a phase), which is the *wh*-phrase. However, the *wh*-phrase itself is still accessible to the higher phasal head, namely N. After X enters the structure, NP is activated for phasal edgehood movement; the *wh*-phrase then moves to SpecNP. D will induce the spell-out of the PP (PP being a phasal complement), but the *wh*-phrase will still be available for movement outside of the NP.

Note that (46) is still ruled out: when the higher *of* is merged in (46), the complement of the D phasal head is sent to spell-out. Since this happens before the *wh*-phrase moves to the edge of the DP phase, the *wh*-phrase cannot move out of this spell-out domain.

(46) ?*Who_i did you see enemies [_PP of [_DP [_XP [_NP t_i friends [_PP of t_i]]]]]?

In light of the above discussion, (34) then needs to be modified. We have seen that the system argued for here deduces a slightly weaker version of (34), which is empirically more adequate than (34): in a configuration where a phasal head takes a phase as its complement, extraction is banned from the complement of the lower phasal head, but the complement itself can move. I therefore modify (34) as follows, also upgrading the relevant constraint to a theorem, to reflect its deduction.

(47) The Phase-over-Phase Theorem
In a double-phase configuration, extraction is banned from the complement of the lower phase.

An important remark is in order at this point though. As noted in footnote 3, Bošković (2015a) and Bošković (2015b) present alternative accounts of the Generalized Complex XP Constraint. The account presented in this paper adopts the same approach to phases as the accounts presented in Bošković (2015a,b); still, theoretically it is rather different from the accounts presented in Bošković (2015a,b). The account presented in Bošković (2015a) crucially relies on a treatment of successive-cyclic movement where successive-cyclic movement involves either creation of unlabeled projections or adjunction (thus, movement targetting the embedded CP in (3) involves either creation of an unlabeled object or adjunction to the embedded CP); antilocality also plays an important role in the account presented in Bošković (2015a). This is not the case with the analysis presented here. Successive-cyclic movement can proceed via SpecCP and antilocality was not needed in the analysis presented above. Also, the analysis presented in Bošković (2015b) is rather different from the analysis presented here in that the analysis presented in Bošković (2015b) crucially relies on the assumption that what is sent to spell-out is the phase itself, not the complement of a phasal head, while the analysis presented here adopts phasal head complement spell-out.

However, it should be pointed out that the analysis presented here differs from Bošković (2015a,b) in one empirical respect. Under the analysis of extraction from double-phase configurations presented here, extraction from the lower phase in a double-phase configuration is actually not banned for elements that are base-generated at the edge of the lower phase, like K in

(48) (where XP and YP are phases).[17]

(48) [$_{XP}$ [$_{X'}$[$_{YP}$ K [$_{YP/Y'}$

In all the unacceptable cases of extraction out of double-phase configurations discussed above, the problem arose with movement to the edge of the lower phase (hence only for elements base-generated within the complement of the lower phase) because the merger of the higher phasal head was making that movement impossible. Since the movement to the edge of the lower phase was blocked, movement out of the lower phase was blocked too, the former being a prerequisite for the latter. No problem (at least not with respect to the locality issues discussed here) would then arise if the extracted element is base-generated at the edge of the lower phase—merger of the higher phasal head would have no effect on it; it would still be accessible for movement to a higher position.

Bošković (2015a,b) does present several unacceptable cases that are analyzed as involving the configuration where the extracted element is base-generated at the edge of the lower phase, as in the following examples involving *combien*-extraction in French, taken from Bošković (2015b). (49)–(50) show that simple *combien*-extraction, where the DP from which *combien*-extraction takes place is a verbal complement, is allowed (49), while deep *combien*-extraction, where the relevant DP is a complement of a noun, is not (50).

(49) Combien$_i$ a-t-il consulté [$_{DP}$ t$_i$ de livres]?
how-many has-he consulted of books

(50)?*Combien$_i$ a-t-il consulté [$_{DP}$ (plusieurs/des) préfaces [$_{DP}$ t$_i$
how-many has-he consulted several/some prefaces
de livres]]
of books
'How many books did he consult several/some prefaces of?'

If examples like (50) (and other cases of this sort from Bošković 2015a,b) are to be analyzed as involving the same kind of locality effect as the ones discussed earlier in section 3.2,[18] *combien* would not be generated at the

---

[17] The analysis given in Bošković (2015b) blocks such extraction; the account developed in Bošković (2015a) blocks it for YP-adjuncts, but not necessarily for all YP-Specs.

[18] To determine whether this should be done (i.e., whether we are dealing with the same effect here), it may be worth checking *combien*-extraction with ergative verbs. The

edge of the DP; it would be generated in a lower position (i.e., within the complement of D) and move to SpecDP in constructions where it undergoes movement out of the DP. The above discussion would then straightforwardly extend to this case.

Alternatively, if *combien* is generated in SpecDP, antilocality could be appealed to; in fact, (50) would be ruled out by antilocality in the current system if Erlewine's (2016) approach to antilocality, where A'-movement from SpecXP must cross a phrase other than XP to satisfy antilocality, is adopted; or we could assume that *combien* is generated adjoined to DP, with antilocality requiring that movement crosses a full phrase, not just a segment (see Bošković 2013a; note, however, that, in contrast to Bošković (2015a), where antilocality plays a major role in the deduction of the Complex XP Constraint, the account presented above did not otherwise need to appeal to antilocality).

At any rate, I leave examining in more detail the configuration in question for future research. What is important to note here is that, as long as nothing else is interferring, the current analysis bans successive-cyclic movement through the lower phase in a double-phase configuration; it does not ban all extraction from the lower phase. This will actually be taken advantage of in section 5, where another acceptable case of movement from the lower phase will be presented; that section will also sharpen the relevant notion of successive-cyclic movement.[19]

---

situation is, however, not completely clear here. There is some locality effect, but it is quite weak, as illustrated by the following examples provided by Amélie Rocquet (p.c.) (the same holds for the inversion strategy for *wh*-questions; note that the degradation is slightly stronger with the passive counterpart of (i), see here footnote 9).

(i) Combien$_i$ il a consulté [$_{DP}$ t$_i$ de livres]?
    how-many he has consulted of books
    'He consulted how many books?'

(ii) ?Combien$_i$ il est arrivé [$_{DP}$ t$_i$ de livres]?
    how-many there is arrived of books
    'There arrived how many books?'

[19] The case in question will actually involve movement from the complement of the lower phase in a double-phase configuration, which will, however, be shown to be allowed in that particular context under the current deduction of (47) (see in this respect footnote 29; for ease of exposition, below I will put aside the exceptional context in question unless it is directly relevant and will keep referring to (47)).

4 Phase Collapsing

Bošković (2015a) observes one context in which the CNPC effect is voided, involving what is refered to as phase collapsing in that work. In this section I discuss one relevant case of this type, showing that the current analysis can also capture the phase-collapsing effect.

A number of Bantu languages do not display Complex NP Constraint effects, as illustrated by the Setswana example in (51), taken from Bošković (2015a).

(51) Ke m-ang yo o utlw-ile-ng ma-gatwe a
 it C1-who C1REL 2SGSM hear-PERF-REL C6-rumor C6SM
 gore ntša e lom-ile?
 that C9-dog C9SM bite-PERF
 'Who did you hear rumors that a dog bit?'

As in other Bantu languages, in Setswana the noun always precedes all other NP-elements, which is analyzed in terms of N-to-D movement (see Carstens 2010 on the N-to-D analysis of the N-initial word order in Bantu). I argue that this is what is responsible for the lack of the Complex NP Constraint effect in Setswana.

Consider the configuration in (52), where X and Y are phasal heads.

(52) [$_{XP}$ Y$_i$+X [$_{YP}$ t$_i$ K]]

Bošković (2015a) proposes that in the case of a complex phase, that is, a phasal projection that is headed by two phasal heads (due to the head-movement of the lower phasal head to the higher phasal head), we are dealing with phase collapsing, that is, the two phases are collapsed into one. Since we are dealing with one phase in such contexts (YP not being a phase), this means that the complement of Y is not sent to spell-out in (52) (note that I assume that there is a feature on Y and X which drives the movement in question; this feature indicates that the phasehood of YP will be voided hence K is not sent to spell-out when Y enters the structure).[20]

The exceptional behavior of Setswana with respect to the Complex NP

---

[20] While phase collapsing is somewhat similar to phase sliding/extension (see den Dikken 2007, Gallego and Uriagereka 2007, Wurmbrand 2013a), where head movement extends the phase to the next projection, it is actually a much more constrained mechanism (note that it arises only when a phasal head moves to a phasal head) with very different empirical effects; see Bošković (2015a) for a comparison.

Constraint can be captured under phase collapsing given that Setswana has N-to-D movement, as indicated by the N-initial nature of DPs in Setswana. As a result of N-to-D movement, the object DP in (51) is a complex phasal domain, headed by two phasal heads, D and N. (I assume that XP from the earlier discussion of English is either not present in Setswana, or it is present, with X undergoing movement to D and N moving to the X+D head.)[21] Since we are dealing here with one phase, the NP is not a phase, hence it does not induce spell-out. This means that the N does not cause spell-out for its CP complement, hence *wh*-movement out of the CP is possible. Since the first phasal head above the embedded CP in (51) is D, the complement of the CP will not be sent to spell-out before D is merged. Given that there is at least one non-phase between CP and DP (NP; as noted above, XP may also be present in this domain), the *wh*-phrase can move to the edge of the CP phase before D enters the structure, that is, before the spell-out of the C-complement. The *wh*-phrase is then available for movement to SpecDP.

Bošković (2015a) discusses a number of other cases of phase collapsing. All of them can be captured by the contextual phasehood analysis argued for here. As an illustration, consider one such case from Galician.

Galician has a rather interesting phenomenon of D-to-V incorporation which, as demonstrated in Uriagereka (1988, 1996) and Bošković (2013b), voids islandhood effects. As an illustration of the island-voiding effect of D-to-V incorporation, consider the specificity effect. Like English, Galician disallows movement from definite NPs, as in (53a). However, the violation is voided when the head of the DP incorporates into the verb, as (53b) shows.[22]

(53) a. *e   de quén$_i$ viche   o   retrato t$_i$?
         and of who   saw(you) the   portrait
     b. e   de quén$_j$ viche-lo$_i$ [$_{DP}$ [$_{D'}$ t$_i$ [$_{NP}$ retrato t$_j$]]]?
         and of whom   saw(you)-the   portrait
        'so, who have you seen the portrait of?'
        (Uriagereka 1988)

Regarding (53a), a definite DP island effect, I simply assume that a definite D cannot work as an attractor (i.e., movement to SpecDP is not possible

---

[21] Note that Bošković (2015a) assumes that in the phase-collapsing configuration, the moved phase head must be a sister to a segment of the higher phase head.

[22] Note that I assume that V moves to v, and D incorporates into the V+v head. Since traces do not count as interveners (see Chomsky 1995; see also Bošković 2011 for an account of the generalization), there is no locality violation here.

here), whatever the reason for that is. Since the wh-phrase then cannot move to the edge of DP, it is not available for movement out of the DP, given the PIC.

Consider now (53b). As a result of D-movement, vP is a complex phasal domain, which means that DP does not function as a phase here. The merger of v causes the spell-out for the NP phase, that is, it triggers the spell-out of the N-complement. However, given the above approach to spell-out/the PIC, v can still attract the complement of N (even if we assume that the complement cannot move to SpecNP). The analysis thus unifies the contrast in (53) with the lack of the CNPC effect in Setswana (51).[23] The other cases of phase collapsing discussed in Bošković (2015a) can also be captured under the approach to phases argued for here.

5 Infinitives

I now turn to infinitives, which raise a number of interesting issues.

Consider first control infinitives.[24] Adjunct extraction is banned from non-verbal control infinitival complements, as illustrated by (54).

(54) a. *How did he witness an [$_{NP}$ attempt [to fix the car t]]?
 b. *How is John [$_{AP}$ able [to fix the car t]]?
 c. *How is it [$_{AP/NP}$ possible/time [to fix the car t]]?

Such cases instantiate the general pattern of the Complex XP Constraint/Phase-over-Phase configuration and can be accounted for in the same way as other such cases discussed above.

It is standardly assumed that control infinitives are phases. Then, *how* has to move to the edge of the infinitive to be able to move out of it. However, since the head merged with the infinitive in (55), which gives the structure of (54a–b), is a phasal head, the complement of Inf is sent to spell-out before the wh-phrase is able to move to the edge of the infinitive. (InfP

---

[23] As noted in Bošković (2015a), D-incorporation does not rescue CNPC violations in Galician, which is expected: what is responsible for the CNPC effect is the phasehood of NP, which is not affected by D-incorporation.

[24] Since some islands are completely weakened with argument extraction out of infinitives (this is, e.g., the case with wh-islands; for most speakers of English argument extraction out of wh-infinitives is fully acceptable, while adjunct extraction is disallowed even from infinitival wh-islands), in what follows I will focus on adjunct extraction (for another interfering factor that arises with argument but not adjunct extraction out of infinitives which is related to phase collapsing, see Bošković 2015a).

is used for ease of exposition, it stands for whatever the category of the infinitive is; see Wurmbrand 2014 for relevant discussion.)

(55) a. *How$_i$ did he witness an [$_{NP}$ attempt [$_{InfP}$ to fix the car t$_i$]]
b. *How$_i$ is John [$_{AP}$ able [$_{InfP}$ to fix the car t$_i$]]

Consider now raising infinitives. Li (2003) observes that, in contrast to examples like (54), adjunct extraction is allowed out of raising infinitives, that is, *how* can modify the infinitive in (56).

(56) How is John likely [to fix the car t]?

This is expected in Chomsky's (2000) phasal system, where control infinitives are phases, but raising infinitives are not, the reason for this difference being that control infinitives are CPs while raising infinitives are IPs, and only CPs are phases. *How* can then move from the infinitive in (56). However, in Bošković (2014), where the highest clausal projection is a phase, the infinitive in both (54) and (56) is a phase regardless of whether it is IP or CP (for relevant discussion, see here Wurmbrand 2013b, 2014). At first sight, (56) seems to favor Chomsky's position. However, a closer scrutiny reveals that adjunct extraction from raising infinitives is impossible.

A number of authors have argued that traditional raising infinitives are actually ambiguous between the raising and the control option (see, e.g., Lasnik and Saito 1992, Martin 2001). There are several ways to disambiguate such infinitives, the most straightforward one being to use expletive *there*: since expletive *there* cannot function as a controller it is incompatible with the control option. Surprisingly, such disambiguation affects extraction. Thus, the embedded reading of *how* is not available in (57) (i.e., it is much more difficult to get it in (57) than in (56); the grammaticality judgments are indicated only for the embedded clause reading of the adjunct in (57)–(58)).

(57) a. *How$_i$ is there likely [to arrive someone t$_i$ tomorrow]?
b. *How$_i$ does there seem [to have arrived someone t$_i$]?

Idiom chunks behave like expletives in this respect: the embedded-clause reading is not available in (58).[25]

---

[25] It should be noted here that since there are verbs that disallow expletive subjects and scope ambiguities from (59) but still allow idiom chunks as subjects (see, e.g., Zubizarreta 1983, Rochette 1988), idiom chunks are not a fully reliable diagnostic of raising.

(58) *How$_i$ is the hatchet likely [to be buried t$_i$]/advantage likely [to be taken of Mary t$_i$]?

Consider also the scopal interaction in the examples in (59)–(61).

(59) Some senator is likely to lie to every member of his committee.

(60) Some senator tried to lie to every member of his committee.

(61) How$_i$ is some senator likely [to lie to every member of his committee t$_i$]?

(59) is ambiguous but (60) is not: the subject must take wide scope in (60) (i.e., in contrast to (59), the embedded clause object cannot take wide scope in (60)). (59)–(60) illustrate the well-known raising/control difference regarding scope (see May 1985). Significantly, the subject must take wide scope in (61), where *how* is extracted from the embedded clause (the low scope reading of the subject is more difficult to get in (61) than in (59) on the embedded clause reading of *how*), which confirms that adjunct extraction forces the control option.

These facts all follow if the highest clausal projection is a phase regardless of its category. This makes both control and raising infinitives phases. Martin (2001) argues that *seem* assigns subject θ-role on the control option (see Martin 2001 for discussion of the nature of this θ-role). There is then a vP above VP on the control option, as in (62). No problem regarding extraction arises here. On the other hand, on the raising option, external θ-role is not assigned. This means that (θ-marking) vP is not present, hence adjunct extraction is disallowed, (63) involving a phase-over-phase configuration (with phases given in boldface).[26]

(62) How$_i$ did John [$_{vP}$ [$_{VP}$ seem [$_{Infinitive}$ PRO to have hit Bill t$_i$]]]?

(63) *How$_i$ does there [$_{vP}$ seem [$_{Infinitive}$ to have arrived someone t$_i$]]?

Note that these facts confirm the existence of the Generalized Complex VP Constraint which holds only for the contexts where the verb does not assign the external θ-role.

An important question now arises regarding the subject of constructions

---

[26] The analysis can be extended to *likely*, *likely* being verbalized on the control option with the external θ-role assigned in a separate thematic projection on a par with verbs (see Bošković 2015a).

involving ambiguous raising/control predicates like *seem* and *likely*. Given that predicates like *likely* and *seem* are ambiguous between control and raising, it appears that the simplest situation when it comes to subjects would be that such predicates are always control predicates when they have a non-lexical subject (which means such subjects would not be moving from the infinitive), and raising predicates when they have an expletive subject; there would then be no ambiguous constructions, each *likely/seem* construction would be unambiguously raising or control. This, however, will not work because of examples like (59), which contrasts with (60) in that the embedded clause quantifier can take wide scope. The raising option, which allows scopal reconstruction of the subject, must then be available here. This is confirmed by idiom chunk examples like (58), where the matrix subject should be generated in, hence moving from, the embedded clause, while the adjunct is not allowed to move from inside the infinitive, as discussed above. In contrast to A'-movement, A-movement of the subject is apparently possible out of raising infinitives. This presents us with a rather interesting situation, since A-movement is normally more local than A'-movement.[27]

How can we then account for the fact that subjects can move out of raising infinitives, although A'-movement out of such infinitives is not possible? This can actually be done rather straightforwardly. Let us adopt the standard assumptions that raising infinitives are TPs, with the predicates taking such infinitives as complements lacking thematic vP/aP.[28] As the highest projection in the infinitival clause, this TP will be a phase. I also adopt Chomsky's (2000) assumption (but see Bošković 2007) that the infinitival head undergoes Agree with the infinitival subject which is followed by movement of the subject to the infinitival SpecTP, motivated by the EPP

---

[27] On object A'-movement out of such infinitives, see Bošković (2015a). As noted there, while the situation is less clear in the case of objects (especially given the general infinitival island-weakening effect, see footnote 24), they seem to pattern with adjuncts, modulo the difference in the strength of the violation. For alternative accounts of the A/A'-movement contrast with respect to extraction out of raising infinitives, see Bošković (2015a), who suggests two accounts, one based on feature sharing between the infinitival subject and T and one involving phase-collapsing, and Bošković (2015b), who suggests an account based on the presence of a dummy linker-like projection between the raising AP/VP and the infinitive.

[28] There is plenty of evidence that there is more than one functional projection in the inflectional domain (see, e.g., Bošković 2015a and references therein); I also assume this to be the case. What I am referring to here as TP is the highest functional projection in this domain (I will in fact interchangably use the terms TP and IP below).

property of the infinitive. What is important here is that when it comes to subjects, movement to the edge of the infinitive is not driven by the need to undergo successive-cyclic movement without violating the PIC, which I have refered to above as the phasal edgehood property. Subject movement to the edge of the infinitive is independent of phasal edgehood. Now, above I have suggested that only unambiguous phrases can be phases, which means that XP functions as a phase only after it is merged with another element, with that other element projecting. Due to its nature, phasal edgehood can drive movement only after XP becomes a phase, that is, after the embedding of XP. This is, however, not the case with subject movement to the Spec of the infinitive; this movement is driven independently by a formal property of the infinitival head which has nothing to do with phasal edgehood or the status of the infinitive as a phase. As a result, the subject can move to the Spec of the infinitive before the infinitive is embedded into other structure. This means that when V/A is merged with the infinitive, which leads to the immediate spell-out of the complement of the infinitival head, the subject is located at the edge of the infinitive hence is available for further movement. This is, however, not the case with adjuncts (i.e., A'-movement). Movement of adjuncts to the edge of the infinitive can only be driven by phasal edgehood. However, phasal edgehood cannot drive movement before further embedding of the infinitive. Since in this particular case the embedding immediately triggers spell-out within the infinitive, adjuncts (i.e., a phrase that contains them) are sent to spell-out before they get a chance to move to the edge of the infinitive. The exceptional behavior of subjects in raising contexts is thus captured.[29]

The above discussion also resolves a potential issue that could arise in matrix clauses, for example with respect to the timing of *wh*-movement in (64).

(64) *What$_i$ did [$_{IP}$ John buy t$_i$]?

If movement of *what* in (64) were driven by phasal edgehood, CP could not be the highest projection in (64); rather it would have to be embedded in phonologically null structure, so that it could drive movement of *what* via

---

[29] Note that the above account of raising takes advantage of the fact that the proposed deduction of (47) does leave very narrow room for extraction to take place out of the complement of the lower phase in a double-phase configuration. (For ease of exposition I will, however, keep referring to (47) below.)

phasal edgehood. Given the above discussion of infinitives, this is not necessary. *Wh*-movement of *what* in (64) is independent of phasal edgehood, it is driven by essentially the same considerations as the movement of the subject to the Spec of the infinitive (a strong +*wh*-feature of C in Chomsky's 1993 terms in this case), hence it can occur as soon as the C is merged into the structure.[30]

6 Another Phase-over-Phase Configuration: Phase as a Spec of a Phase

The discussion above has focused on the context where a phasal head takes a phase as its complement, given in (65).

(65) [$_{XP}$ [$_{X'}$ [$_{YP}$ ...]]]

In this section I will briefly explore the consequences of the current proposals for another context where the first maximal projection that dominates a phase is also a phase, namely, the configuration where a phase is the Spec of a phasal projection, a configuration that under standard assumptions in fact arises quite often. The question to be addressed is what consequences the proposals made here have for extraction out of YP in (66), where both XP and YP are phases.

(66) [$_{XP}$ [$_{YP}$ ...] [$_{X'}$]]

Recall that what is at the heart of the current account of (47) is the precise timing of spell-out: Complement of phase X is sent to spell-out when the next phasal head is merged into the structure. In (66), the first merger of YP is not a merger with a head at all, as in all other cases discussed above; it is a merger with another phrase, that is, a projection of a head. If we take the above assumption that spell-out for phase XP is triggered by the merger of the next phasal head literally, then merger of the next phasal head but not merger of a projection of a phasal head will trigger spell-out. This means that the merger of YP with X′ (actually XP at the point of merger) will not trigger spell-out for phase YP. As a result, all else being equal, movement

---

[30] It is a standard assumption that independently of the usual assumptions regarding spell-out domains, where only phasal complements are sent to spell-out, matrix clauses, which are phases, are sent to spell-out. However this is to be implemented it should be extendable to the current system (see, however, Bošković 2015b for an account where this assumption can be dispensed with).

out of YP should be possible;[31] more precisely, nothing proposed above would rule it out. Merger of YP into the structure will activate YP for phasal edgehood movement. Movement to the edge of YP will then take place before another phasal head enters the structure, triggering spell-out for phase YP. On the other hand, if even merger with a projection of a phasal head triggers spell-out, YP in (66) will be impervious to extraction (for elements located within its complement) for the same reason a phase that functions as a phasal complement is. In this scenario, in a configuration where the first maximal projection that dominates a phase is a phase, regardles of whether the dominated phase is the complement or the Spec of the dominating phase, extraction will be possible only for the immediate constituents of the dominated phase, that is, its Spec and its complement. The upshot of this is that the current analysis does not make a clear prediction regarding extraction from phase YP in (66); the extraction can be (in principle) allowed or disallowed.

It would be way beyond the scope of this paper to determine whether extraction in the context in question is indeed possible—extraction out of Specs is a notoriously murky issue, affected by many factors that are independent of those considered in this paper (i.e., the main proposal in (37) and the question of the timing of spell-out discussed above). I merely note here one relevant case: extraction from a subject of a transitive (non-ergative) construction that is located in its base-generated position in SpecvP. Assuming that vP, the highest projection in the thematic domain, is a phase here, and that the subject is a DP, hence a phase, the context in question involves the configuration in (66), as should be obvious from (67).

(67) [$_{vP}$ [$_{DP}$ Subject] [$_{v'}$]]

The question is then whether extraction is possible out of the subject in the configuration in question. It is often assumed that it is; in this respect see for example the language survey in Stepanov (2001, 2007). As discussed above,

---

[31] However, it is not completely clear that everything else is equal. Thus, if correct, Hiraiwa's (2005) claim that the edge of the edge of a phase is not accessible from the outside, which is captured by the formulation of the PIC in (43), may make extraction from within the Spec of a phasal head independently impossible (though the PIC could be re-defined in such a way that this issue does not arise (i.e., without taking into consideration Hiraiwa's claim) but a phasal complement is still accessible from the outside). However, the issue in question would not arise if, as suggested above, all we have is the assumption that the internal structure of what is sent to spell-out is inaccessible in the syntax, the PIC being eliminated.

this can be straightforwardly captured if only merger of the next phasal head (not merger with a projection of a phasal head) triggers spell-out. It should, however, be noted that the issue of extraction out of subjects located in SpecvP is not completely settled. Thus, Uriagereka (2012) claims that extraction is in fact disallowed in the context in question (and out of Specs more generally).

Somewhat related is the issue of extraction from extraposed clauses. Extraposed clauses exhibit varied behavior with respect to extraction. Some extraposed clauses disallow it, like (68) and (54c), which can be easily captured under the current analysis.

(68) *How$_i$ is it possible [that John will fix the car t$_i$]?

However, at least for some speakers, some extraposed clauses do allow extraction, as in (69).[32]

(69) How$_i$ is it likely [$_{CP}$ (that) John fixed the car t$_i$]?

Bošković (2015a) explores two alternative accounts of examples like (69), which can be adjusted to the current system. Extraposed CPs have been argued to be Specs/adjuncts (see, e.g., Reinhart 1980, Stowell 1981, Bošković 2002). Assume that this is indeed the case for the extraposed clauses in question, that is, for those that allow extraction.[33] If only merger of the next phasal head, not merger of a projection of a phasal head, triggers spell-out, since the extraposed clauses in question are merged with a projection of A/V, not with A/V, their merger into the structure will not trigger spell-out for the CP phase; that is, the IP complement of the extraposed CP phase will not

---

[32] Subject extraction is still disallowed, as in *who$_i$ is it likely t$_i$ fixed the car; see Bošković (2015a, 2016) for alternative accounts of this fact.

[33] If, as discussed in Bošković (2015a) and Zaring (1994), expletives can be generated either within AP/VP or outside of AP/VP, we can take generation of the expletive in the complement position of A/V to lead to the placement of the clause in the VP/AP-Spec/adjunct position. The varied behavior of extraposed clauses regarding extraction (some of them allow extraction (69), and some of them do not (68); see Bošković 2015a and references therein) can then be tied to whether or not the expletive is generated within AP/VP (it would be in (69) but not in (68)). Interestingly, in some languages (e.g., French and Dutch), this difference even has a morphological reflex, with the varried behavior of extraposed clauses regarding extraction being correlated with morphologically different expletives (see Bennis 1986, Bošković 2015a, Zaring 1994; under this analysis, English would also have two different types of expletives which would correlate with different extraction possibilities, they would just happen to have the same morphological realization in English, see Bošković 2015a).

be sent to spell-out upon the merger of the extraposed CP into the structure. *How* can then move to the SpecCP of the extraposed clause in (69) before the IP of the extraposed clause is sent to spell-out. After the next phasal head, namely matrix C, is introduced into the structure, the IP of the extraposed CP will be sent to spell-out but *how* will still be available for movement outside of the extraposed CP.

However, Bošković (2015a) also gives an alternative analysis of (69) which has no bearing on the issue of whether merger with a projection of a phasal head triggers spell-out. Under that analysis, which also assumes that what is behind the varried behavior of extraposed clauses with respect to extraction is whether the expletive is generated within or outside of AP/VP (see footnote 33), following the line of research in Moro (1997), Hornstein and Witkoś (2003), and Sabel (2000), expletives that are generated AP/VP-internally, which is the case with (69), form a constituent with its associate clause. In particular, the two are generated within a dummy linker-like projection FP, as the Spec and the complement of that non-phasal projection.[34] Under the current analysis, the merger of the CP with F will activate the CP for phasal edgehood movement so that the wh-phrase can move to the edge of the CP before the adjective is merged into the structure, triggering spell-out for the CP phase.

7 Conclusion

Taking as the starting point the well-known fact that extraction from Complex NPs is banned while extraction from Complex VPs is allowed, we have seen that the former represents a pervasive pattern found in many contexts, while the latter is highly exceptional. Thus, not only clausal but all complements of nouns are resistant to extraction. Furthermore, adjectives, prepositions, and ergative verbs pattern with nouns—their complements are also resistant to extraction regardless of their categorial status. The only context where extraction from the complement of a lexical head is freely allowed involves non-ergative verbs. Adopting an approach to phases where the highest projection in the thematic domain of a lexical head as well as the highest projection in the non-thematic/functional domain function as phases,

---

[34] This may actually be den Dikken's (2006) RelatorP under Moro's (1997) expletive/CP-constituent analysis, where the expletive and the CP are generated as a small clause involving a predication relation.

I have restated the ban on extraction from complements of lexical heads (the Complex XP Constraint) as a ban on extraction in double-phase configurations (where a phase head takes a phase as its complement), more precisely, as a ban on extraction from the complement of the lower phase head in a double-phase configuration, also proposing a deduction of the ban in question (and exploring some of its consequences).

In the spirit of contextual approaches to phasehood, where the phasal status of X is generally determined after X is embedded into larger structure, and the assumption that only phrases can function as phases, where under the Bare Phrase Structure framework the phrasal status of X can be unambiguously determined only after X is embedded into larger structure, I have argued that XP functions as a phase only after it is merged into the structure, with movement to the edge of XP driven by the need to undergo successive-cyclic movement without violating the PIC taking place after this merger. Since merger with a phasal head triggers immediate spell-out of the complement of the lower phasal head, movement from the complement of phase XP is possible only if the first head merged with XP is then not a phasal head. In Complex XP Constraint configurations, the first merged head is a phasal head, that is, we are dealing here with a phase-over-phase configuration, which is recalcitrant to extraction. However, while the complement of the lower phasal head is recalcitrant to extraction in the configuration in question, the complement itself can be extracted, which was also shown to follow from the phasal system adopted here.

References

Abels, Klaus. 2003. Successive cyclicity, anti-locality, and adposition stranding. Doctoral dissertation, University of Connecticut, Storrs.
Bach, Emmon, and George Horn. 1976. Remarks on 'Conditions on Transformations'. *Linguistic Inquiry* 7:265–299.
Belletti, Adriana, and Luigi Rizzi. 1988. Psych-verbs and theta theory. *Natural Language and Linguistic Theory* 6:291–352.
Bennis, Hans. 1986. *Gaps and dummies*. Dordrecht: Foris.
Boeckx, Cedric. 2005. Some notes on bounding. Ms., Harvard University, Cambridge, MA.
Bošković, Željko. 1994. D-structure, theta-criterion, and movement into theta-positions. *Linguistic Analysis* 24:247–286.
Bošković, Željko. 1995. Case properties of clauses and the Greed principle. *Studia Linguistica* 49:32–53.
Bošković, Željko. 2002. A-movement and the EPP. *Syntax* 5:167–218.

Bošković, Željko. 2007. On the locality and motivation of Move and Agree: An even more minimal theory. *Linguistic Inquiry* 38:589–644.

Bošković, Željko. 2011. Rescue by PF deletion, traces as (non)interveners, and the that-trace effect. *Linguistic Inquiry* 42:1–44.

Bošković, Željko. 2012. On NPs and clauses. In *Discourse and grammar: From sentence types to lexical categories*, ed. by Günther Grewendorf and Thomas Ede Zimmermann, 179–242. Berlin: Mouton de Gruyter.

Bošković, Željko. 2013a. Phases beyond clauses. In *The nominal structure in Slavic and beyond*, ed. by Lilia Schürcks, Anastasia Giannakidou, and Urtzi Etxeberria, 75–128. Berlin: de Gruyter.

Bošković, Željko. 2013b. Traces do not head islands: What can PF deletion rescue? In *Deep insights, broad perspectives*, ed. by Yoichi Miyamoto, Daiko Takahashi, Hideki Maki, Masao Ochi, Koji Sugisaki, and Asako Uchibori, 56–93. Tokyo: Kaitakusha.

Bošković, Željko. 2014. Now I'm a phase, now I'm not a phase. *Linguistic Inquiry* 45:27–89.

Bošković, Željko. 2015a. From the Complex NP Constraint to everything: On deep extractions across categories. *The Linguistic Review* 32:603–669.

Bošković, Željko. 2015b. Deducing the Generalized XP Constraint from phasal spell-out. In *Slavic languages in the perspective of formal grammar: Proceedings of FDSL 10.5, Brno 2014*, ed. by Markéta Ziková, Pavel Caha, and Mojmír Dočekal, 79–100. Bern: Peter Lang.

Bošković, Željko. 2015c. On the ban on movement out of moved elements in the phasal/labeling system. Ms., University of Connecticut, Storrs.

Bošković, Željko. 2016. On the timing of labeling: Deducing Comp-trace effects, the Subject Condition, the Adjunct Condition, and tucking in from labeling. *The Linguistic Review* 33:17–66.

Carstens, Vicki. 2010. Head-movement in Bantu DPs. Paper presented at the 41st annual meeting of the North East Linguistic Society, University of Pensylvania, 22–24 October.

Cheng, Hsu-Te. 2012. Ellipsis: Its correlates with phases and movement. Paper presented at GLOW 35, University of Potsdam.

Chomsky, Noam. 1973. Conditions on transformations. In *A festschrift for Morris Halle*, ed. by Stephen R. Anderson and Paul Kiparsky, 232–286. New York: Holt, Rinehart and Winston.

Chomsky, Noam. 1986. *Barriers*. Cambridge, MA: MIT Press.

Chomsky, Noam. 1993. A minimalist program for linguistic theory. In *The view from Building 20: Essays in Linguistics in Honor of Sylvain Bromberger*, ed. Kenneth Hale and Samuel J. Keyser, 1–52. Cambridge, MA: MIT Press.

Chomsky, Noam. 1995. *The minimalist program*. Cambridge, MA: MIT Press.

Chomsky, Noam. 2000. Minimalist inquiries. In *Step by step*, ed. by Roger Martin, David Michaels, and Juan Uriagereka, 89–155. Cambridge, MA: MIT Press.

Chomsky, Noam. 2001. Derivation by phase. In *Ken Hale: A life in language*, ed. by Michael Kenstowicz, 1–52. Cambridge, MA: MIT Press.

Chomsky, Noam. 2013. Problems of projection. *Lingua* 130:33–49.
Chomsky, Noam. 2015. Problems of projection: Extensions. In *Structures, strategies and beyond: Studies in honour of Adriana Belletti*, ed. by Elisa Di Domenico, Cornelia Hamann, and Simona Matteini, 3–16. Amsterdam/Philadelphia: John Benjamins.
Cinque, Guglielmo. 1990. *Types of A'-dependencies*. Cambridge, MA: MIT Press.
Dikken, Marcel den. 2006. *Relators and linkers: The syntax of predication, predicate inversion and copulas*. Cambridge, MA: MIT Press.
Dikken, Marcel den. 2007. Phase extension: Contours of a theory of the role of head movement in phrasal extraction. *Theoretical Linguistics* 33:1–41.
Erlewine, Michael. 2016. Anti-locality and optimality in Kaqchikel agent focus. *Natural Language and Linguistic Theory* 34:429–479.
Gallego, Ángel, and Juan Uriagereka. 2007. Conditions on sub-extraction. In *Coreference, modality, and focus*, ed. by Luis Eguren and Olga Fernández-Soriano, 45–70. Amsterdam: John Benjamins.
Grohmann, Kleanthes. 2003. *Prolific domains*. Amsterdam: John Benjamins.
Harwood, William. 2014. Being progressive is just a phase: Dividing the functional hierarchy. Doctoral dissertation, University of Gent.
Hiraiwa, Ken. 2005. Dimensions of symmetry in syntax: Agreement and clausal architecture. Doctoral dissertation, MIT, Cambridge, MA.
Hornstein, Norbert, and Jacek Witkoś. 2003. Yet another approach to existential constructions. In *Grammar in focus: Festschrift for Christer Platzack*, ed. by Lars-Olof Delsing, Cecilia Falk, Gunlög Josefsson, and Halldór Ármann Sigurðsson. Lund: Lund University, Department of Scandinavian.
Horrocks, Geoffrey, and Melita Stavrou. 1987. Bounding theory and Greek syntax. *Journal of Linguistics* 23:79–108.
Johnson, Kyle. 1991. Object positions. *Natural Language and Linguistic Theory* 9:577–636.
Johnson, Kyle. 1992. Scope and binding theory. *Syntax and Semantics* 26:259–275.
Kang, Jungmin. 2014. On the absence of TP and its consequences: Evidence from Korean. Doctoral dissertation, University of Connecticut, Storrs.
Landau, Idan. 2009. *The locative syntax of experiencers*. Cambridge, MA: MIT Press.
Lasnik, Howard. 1999. *Minimalist analysis*. Oxford: Blackwell.
Lasnik, Howard, and Mamoru Saito. 1992. *Move α*. Cambridge, MA: MIT Press.
Li, Yafei. 1993. Barriers in terms of categories. Paper presented at the 63th annual LSA meeting, Los Angeles.
Martin, Roger. 2001. Null Case and the distribution of PRO. *Linguistic Inquiry* 32:141–166.
Matushansky, Ora. 2005. Going through a phase. In *MIT Working Papers in Linguistics* 49: *Perspectives on Phases*, ed. by Martha McGinnis and Norvin Richards, 157–181. Cambridge, MA: Department of Linguistics, MIT *Working Papers in Linguistics*.
May, Robert. 1985. *Logical form: Its structure and derivation*. Cambridge, MA: MIT Press.

Moro, Andrea. 1997. *The raising of predicates. Predicative noun phrases and the theory of clause structure*. Cambridge: Cambridge University Press.

Nunes, Jairo. 2009. Dummy prepositions and the licensing of null subjects in Brazilian Portuguese. In *Romance languages and linguistic theory: Selected papers from 'Going Romance' Amsterdam 2007*, ed. by Enoch O. Aboh, Elisabeth van der Linden, Josep Quer, and Petra Sleeman, 243–265. Amsterdam: Benjamins.

Nunes, Jairo, and Juan Uriagereka. 2000. Cyclicity and extraction domains. *Syntax* 3:20–43.

Pesetsky, David. 1995. *Zero syntax*. Cambridge, MA: MIT Press.

Rackowski, Andrea, and Norvin Richards. 2005. Phase edge and extraction. *Linguistic Inquiry* 36:565–599.

Reinhart, Tanya. 1980. On the position of extraposed clauses. *Linguistic Inquiry* 11:621–624.

Rochette, Anne. 1988. Semantic and syntactic aspects of Romance sentential. Doctoral dissertation, MIT, Cambridge, MA.

Ross, John Robert. 1967. Constraints on variables in syntax. Doctoral dissertation, MIT, Cambridge, MA.

Sabel, Joachim. 2000. Expletives as features. In *The proceedings of the nineteenth West Coast Conference on Formal Linguistics*, ed. by Roger Billerey and Brook Danielle Lillehaugen, 101–114. Somerville: Cascadilla Press.

Safir, Kenneth. 1985. *Syntactic chains*. Cambridge: Cambridge University Press.

Saito, Mamoru, and Keiko Murasugi. 1999. Subject predication within IP and DP. In *Beyond principles and parameters*, ed. by Kyle Johnson and Ian Roberts, 167–188. Dordrecht: Kluwer.

Sawada, Tsuyoshi. 2015. Pleonastic merger. Doctoral dissertation, University of Connecticut, Storrs.

Stepanov, Arthur. 2001. Cyclic domains in syntactic theory. Doctoral dissertation, University of Connecticut, Storrs.

Stepanov, Arthur. 2007. The end of CED? *Syntax* 10:80–126.

Stepanov, Arthur. 2012. Voiding island effects via head movement. *Linguistic Inquiry* 43:680–693.

Stowell, Timothy. 1981. Origins of phrase structure. Doctoral dissertation, MIT, Cambridge, MA.

Ticio, Emma. 2003. On the structure of DPs. Doctoral dissertation, University of Connecticut, Storrs.

Uriagereka, Juan. 1988. On government. Doctoral dissertation, University of Connecticut, Storrs.

Uriagereka, Juan. 1996. Determiner clitic placement. In *Current issues in comparative grammar*, ed. by Robert Freidin, 257–294. Dordrecht: Kluwer.

Uriagereka, Juan. 1999. Multiple Spell-Out. In *Working minimalism*, ed. by Samuel David Epstein and Norbert Hornstein, 251–282. Cambridge: MIT Press.

Uriagereka, Juan. 2012. *Spell-out and the Minimalist Program*. Oxford: Oxford University Press.

Wurmbrand, Susi. 2013a. QR and selection: Covert evidence for phasehood. In *Proceedings of the 42nd annual meeting of the North East Linguistic Society (NELS 42)*, ed. by Stefan Keine and Shayne Sloggett, 277–290. Amherst: GLSA.
Wurmbrand, Susi. 2013b. Tagalog infinitives: Consequences for the theory of phases, voice marking, and extraction. Ms., University of Connecticut, Storrs.
Wurmbrand, Susi. 2014. Tense and aspect in English infinitives. *Linguistic Inquiry* 45:403–447.
Zaring, Laurie. 1994. On the relationship between subject pronouns and clausal arguments. *Natural Language and Linguistic Theory* 12:515–569.
Zubizarreta, Maria Luisa. 1983. On the notion "Adjunct Subject" and a class of raising predicates. In *Papers in grammatical theory* (MIT Working Papers in Linguistics 5), ed. by Isabelle Haïk and Diane Massam, 195–231. Cambridge, MA: MIT *Working Papers in Linguistics*.

Simplest Merge, Labeling, and A′-Movement of the Subject*

Manabu Mizuguchi

This paper explores the syntax of subject A′-movement under simplest Merge in Minimalism. I submit that a subject *wh*-phrase (more generally, an operator subject) is internally merged only with CP, proposing the Vacuous Movement Hypothesis. A-properties of the subject directly merged in Spec,CP follow from head movement, which I argue is feature climbing from lower heads to higher heads. I demonstrate that head movement qua feature climbing can also deduce lack of EPP effects on T from labeling. Finally, I argue that ECP or *that-trace* effects are deducible from simplest Merge and labeling, showing that EPP and ECP effects on the subject can be explained by simple computation and its interactions with the interface systems.

Keywords: simplest Merge, labeling, subject *wh*-movement, subject EPP, *that-t* effects

1 Introduction

The Minimalist Program has shifted toward simplifying, for both scientific and biological reasons, the richness or complexity of Universal Grammar, UG (unexplained part of S_0) and reducing the properties of language to general principles governing simple/minimal computation (what are sometimes called "third factor" principles) and interface conditions imposed by the Conceptual-Intentional (CI) and Sensory-Motor (SM) systems, with which language is interfaced through mapping components. This shift toward the

---

* An earlier version of this paper was presented at a workshop held at the 32nd Conference of the English Linguistic Society of Japan (Gakushuin University, Japan, November 8, 2014); part of the paper was developed and presented at Workshop in General Linguistics (WIGL) 12 (the University of Wisconsin-Madison, USA, April 12, 2015). I would like to thank the audience at the two meetings as well as Jun Abe for their helpful comments and discussion. As always, remaining errors and inadequacies are solely mine. The research reported in this paper was supported by Dokkyo University under International Research Grant and by Japan Society for the Promotion of Science under Grant-in-Aid for Young Scientists (B) (#24720193).

simplification of UG, which is articulated by *the Strong Minimalist Thesis* (hereafter SMT) (Chomsky 2000, 2004 and his subsequent recent writings), is the cornerstone hypothesis of the current Minimalism and is considered a remarkable feature distinguishing this research program from the others in the tradition of Generative Grammar.

Under the recognition that language is a recursive system with discrete infinity, it has been assumed that the operation *Merge* (an *n-ary* set-formation operation) is an irreducible and bare minimum part of UG. Interacting with third factor principles, Merge is executed most simply, formulated as "simplest Merge" (= (1)).

(1) *Merge(α, β) = {α, β}*

Under simplest Merge, Merge applies freely and any two syntactic objects (SOs) are iteratively paired in such a way that the two SOs merged are left unchanged (that is, Merge satisfies the No-Tampering Condition, NTC). Hence, Merge applies only at the root of derivation, extending existing structures or sets. Moreover, no new objects (traces, indices, labels, etc.) are added in the process of Merge (i.e., Merge meets the Inclusiveness Condition): linear order, labels and projections like CP and TP as well as notions like "Spec," "complement" are not properties of phrase structure or expressions created by simplest Merge.[1, 2] As illustrated in (2), Merge, executed most simply, recursively yields bare expressions (unordered, unidentified/label-free sets).

(2) a. $\{α, β\}$
 b. $\{γ, \{α, β\}\}$
 c. $\{δ, \{γ, \{α, β\}\}\}$
    ⋮

Minimalism assumes that as far as the properties of language are deduced from simplest Merge and its interactions with the interface systems, language

---

[1] In this paper, these terms are used for expository purposes only.
[2] The Inclusiveness Condition can be considered part of NTC: adding new objects will tamper with expressions created by simplest Merge. Reasonably, NTC and the Inclusiveness Condition can be subsumed under a more general condition, which could be called the "Preservation Condition."

 (i) Existing SOs in syntax remain immutable throughout derivations.

For expository purposes, I continue to use the terms, NTC and the Inclusiveness Condition.

will be a perfectly designed system.

The purpose of this paper is to consider the simplest-Merge hypothesis in the syntax of A'-movement (i.e., Internal Merge, IM) of a subject *wh*-phrase (more generally, an operator subject), exploring optimal derivation of subject *wh*-movement and its theoretical and empirical consequences. I submit that a subject *wh*-phrase undergoes vacuous movement to the Spec of TP in the SMT-based Minimalist system: it will be merged with CP but not with TP, there being no Spec,TP created in the derivation of subject *wh*-movement. I show that the proposed derivation will have important consequences for both EPP and ECP effects on the subject, arguing that EPP and ECP can be derived from simplest Merge and labeling (that is, Full Interpretation, one element of principled explanation under SMT).

The organization of the paper is as follows. In section 2, I discuss the derivation of subject *wh*-movement under the SMT assumptions and propose the Vacuous Movement Hypothesis. In section 3, I consider A-properties of the subject and argue that they follow from head movement, which I claim is an upward counterpart to feature inheritance. I also show that this proposal can solve the problem of "EPP" in T. In section 4, I discuss *that-t(race)* effects observed in long-distance subject *wh*-movement, arguing that ECP effects on the subject can be deduced from the Vacuous Movement Hypothesis and head movement qua feature climbing. In section 5, I summarize and conclude the paper.

2 Derivation of Subject *Wh*-Movement

2.1 The Vacuous Movement Hypothesis

Subject *wh*-movement, which I explore in this paper, is most typically illustrated by (3).

(3) Which student read the book?

The subject *which student* is externally merged in Spec,v*P (= (4a)) and is moved (that is, internally merged) in the course of the derivation. For proper interpretation at the interfaces, suppose that all operations (except External Merge, EM) will apply at the phase level under the SMT assumptions. Then, the subject *wh*-phrase will be internally merged not when TP is structured but when the CP phase is created (= (4b)). Given simplest Merge, this suggests that the merge will apply only to CP, with the subject *n*P internally merged with CP but not with TP: since TP is embedded and is not a root of the derivation when the CP phase is yielded, simplest Merge will disallow movement or IM of the subject into Spec,TP; moving into the relevant Spec would require tuck-in/infixation of the subject, violating NTC. Hence, once the CP phase is structured as in (4b), the movement of the subject will go as illustrated in (4c) under simplest Merge.[3]

(4) a. [$_{v*P}$ which student [v^*-read the book]]
　　b. [$_{CP}$ C [$_{TP}$ T [$_{v*P}$ which student [v^*-read the book]..]
　　c. [$_{CP}$ which student [C [$_{TP}$ T [$_{v*P}$ ⟨which student⟩ [v^*-read the book]..]

In (4c), the existing structure is not at all tampered with by the IM.

Notice that Merge, as it applies freely, can indeed move the subject *wh*-phrase to Spec,TP in a way satisfying NTC. Suppose that the subject is internally merged when TP is created as in (5). Then, merge with TP will not tamper with existing structures and can be executed without violating NTC.

(5) a. [$_{v*P}$ which student [v^*-read the book]]
　　b. [$_{TP}$ which student [T [$_{v*P}$ ⟨which student⟩ [v^*-read the book]..]
　　　　　　　　　　　　　　　　　　　　　　　　　　　　IM applies to TP
　　c. [$_{CP}$ which student [C [$_{TP}$ ⟨which student⟩ [T [$_{v*P}$ ⟨which student⟩ [v^*-read the book]..]
　　　　　　　　　　　　　　　　　　　　　　　　　　　　IM applies to CP

This mode of movement, though allowed in principle, will be ruled out extrasyntactically at the interfaces in violation of Full Interpretation. If IM occurs at the non-phase level before Transfer as in (5), occurrences created by IM would be identified as "repetitions" (that is, distinct occurrences of the same SO), and not as "copies" (i.e., non-distinct occurrences of the same SO forming a discontinuous element), which is because the interfaces cannot determine whether the occurrences created are by IM or by EM under the Inclusiveness Condition; on the other hand, if IM applies at the phase level and the information is locally available to the interfaces (or interface components) that an SO is internally merged, then the occurrences created can be identified as copies and hence, interpreted as forming a discontinuous element. As shown in (6), the multiple occurrences of the subject created by the merge in (5) would be identified as distinct at the interfaces and each is independently interpreted. This would result in distinct/non-chain interpreta-

---

[3] Unless otherwise noted, t_i is a copy of the *i*-indexed SO. In this paper, "t_i" and "⟨SO⟩" are used interchangeably as copies of an SO (i.e., lower occurrences of the same SO created by IM).

tions of such occurrences, not a chain interpretation, which would violate Full Interpretation and cause interpretive deviance at the CI interface.[4]

(6) a. [$_{TP}$ which student$_2$ [T [$_{v*P}$ which student$_1$ [v^*-read the book]..]]
   b. [$_{CP}$ which student$_2$ [C [$_{TP}$ ⟨which student$_2$⟩ [T [$_{v*P}$ which student$_1$ [v^*-read the book]..]]   (which student$_2$ ≠ which student$_1$)

Furthermore, the relevant merge at the non-phase level will incur a labeling failure. As we have noted, expressions created by simplest Merge are free from labels and must be labeled for proper interpretation at the CI interface as well as for the rules of externalization (Spell-Out). The Labeling Algorithm (LA) determines the properties of unidentified sets created by simplest Merge through minimal search (Chomsky 2013, 2014a,b, 2015). As we have discussed, the lower occurrence of the subject (represented as *which student$_1$* for expository purposes) will be identified as distinct from its higher occurrences, not being identified as part of a discontinuous element. Thus, it will be visible to LA (Chomsky 2013, 2014a,b, 2015, Ott 2012). This, however, will cause a labeling failure of the α-marked set in (7): the set ({{*which student$_1$*}, {*v*-read the book*}}), which forms an XP-YP structure with the form {{X, ZP}, {Y, WP}}, can only be labeled by minimal detection of agreeing heads; however, *which* and v^* do not agree in their shared ϕ-features and agreeing heads cannot be detected by minimal search LA. Labeling will be ambiguous and the set cannot be labeled by LA.

(7) [$_{CP}$ which student$_2$ [C [$_{TP}$ ⟨which student$_2$⟩ [T [$_α$ which student$_1$ [v^*-read the book]..]]   (α = unlabeled)

The labeling failure will also cause problems for interpretation and externalization at the interfaces.

In summary, the SO derived by applications of IM at the non-phase level cannot be interpreted or externalized properly. The derivation will be properly interpreted and externalized only when the IM of a subject *wh*-phrase applies at the phase level, which, as we have discussed, will exclude

---

[4] (6b) will be externalized (pronounced) as in (i).
   (i) Which student which student read the book?

The externalization is empirically wrong. We should notice, however, that it is phonologically well-formed: the two occurrences of *which student* in (6b) are identified not as copies, which form a single chain, but as distinct occurrences, each of which will be phonologically realized independently. See also our discussion in section 2.4.

internal merge of the subject with TP under simplest Merge.⁵

In this paper, I submit that as a consequence of simplest Merge and its interactions with the interface systems, a subject *wh*-phrase is merged only with CP at the phase level. I propose the syntactic process in (8) as the derivation of subject *wh*-movement, which does not tamper with the existing structure.⁶

(8)   [$_{CP}$ subject$_{wh/operator}$ [C [$_{TP}$ T [$_{v*P}$ ⟨subject$_{wh/operator}$⟩ [v^* [$_{VP}$ ...]..]

In (8), contra the standard assumption, the subject does not move to Spec,TP in subject *wh*-movement. Notice that the proposed analysis does not raise any problems with ϕ-features and EPP: ϕ-features in T can be valued by Agree without establishing a Spec-Head relation; moreover, under simplest Merge, Merge applies freely and there is no EPP, which is simply a stipulation that should be dispensed with (Mizuguchi 2014b). As I argue below, EPP effects are deducible from labeling. I submit that the derivation proposed in (8) is a minimalist version of the "Vacuous Movement Hypothesis." Under the assumptions of SMT, unlike in the traditional hypothesis (Chomsky 1986), the Spec that is not created by the relevant movement is

---

⁵ Mizuguchi (2014a) argues that transfer of TP follows from movement to Spec,TP. Given this argument, subject *wh*-movement will be impossible if the subject *wh*-phrase moves to the relevant Spec before moving to Spec,CP; the *wh*-phrase, along with TP, will be transferred and cannot move from Spec,TP to Spec,CP.

⁶ In this paper, I do not discuss the derivation of subject raising, in which a normal subject is internally merged with TP and moves to the Spec of TP. The interested reader is referred to Chomsky (2008), Epstein, Kitahara, and Seely (2012), Mizuguchi (2014a) and Narita (2014), among others for how counter-cyclic A-movement is executed under NTC. If counter-cyclic A-movement is possible in a way satisfying NTC, then merge of a subject *wh*-phrase with TP at the phase level would be possible in principle. As we noted in the last footnote, assuming Mizuguchi (2014a), this derivational option precludes subject *wh*-movement. We will also discuss one possible illustration of this movement in section 2.4 which could evade this problem. As we will argue there, the relevant derivation will be ruled out as well and an empirically well-formed SO in subject *wh*-movement can only be produced by the derivation proposed in (8).

not Spec,CP, but Spec,TP.[7, 8]

2.2 Vacuous Movement to Spec,TP

In this section, I show that theoretical arguments for the Vacuous Movement Hypothesis are empirically endorsed as well. If a subject *wh*-phrase is not merged with TP and does not move to Spec,TP, then subject *wh*-movement will show different empirical properties than subject raising, in which the subject moves to Spec,TP.[9] I argue with examples from various languages that this is, in fact, the case, showing that the derivation proposed in (8) is empirically supported as well.

2.2.1 Scope of the Subject

First, consider scope relations. As shown in (9), the subject shows different scope relations with an object quantifier depending on whether it is a *wh*-phrase or not (May 1985).

(9) a. Who loves everyone? (*wh* > *every*; *every > *wh*)
    b. Someone likes everyone. (*some* > *every*; *every* > *some*)

Suppose that universal and existential quantifiers raise to take scope at Spec,TP. With this assumption in mind, the unambiguous reading in (9a) will be straightforwardly deduced from the Vacuous Movement Hypothesis. As illustrated in (10a), under the proposed analysis of subject *wh*-movement, the IM of the subject *who* does not create Spec,TP and as a result, the object cannot raise to take scope over the subject at the relevant Spec. In (9b), on the other hand, a normal subject is merged with TP and raises to its Spec.

---

[7] See also Bošković (2014), Erlewine (2014, 2016), Legate (2011, 2014), Miyoshi (2009), Mizuguchi (2013) and Ouali (2008) for independent arguments for (8).

Some may wonder how a subject-predicate relation is warranted if the subject is not merged with TP. I argue that the relation is guaranteed by the fact that the subject is merged with v*P/vP (Narita and Fukui 2014): the merge will yield a subject-predicate relation at the CI interface for the creation of a non-endocentric XP-YP structure with a predicative phrase (i.e., subject-v*P/vP).

[8] Notice that under simplest Merge, a normal subject can also be merged in a way illustrated in (8). The relevant derivation, however, will be ruled out at the interfaces: if the subject in question is merged with CP, forming its Spec, it will incur interpretive problems because it is not an operator and is not in the right position where it can be interpreted properly at the CI interface (i.e., Spec,TP).

[9] In this paper, we simply assume that a normal subject moves to Spec,TP. Again, I leave the discussion of the derivation of subject raising under simplest Merge to the references cited in footnote 6.

Therefore, the object can move over the subject and can take scope over it (= (10b)).

(10) a. [CP who [C [TP everyone [TP T [v*P ⟨who⟩ [v*-likes ⟨everyone⟩]..]
(wh > every)
b. [CP [TP everyone [TP someone [likes ⟨everyone⟩]..] (every > some)
cf. c. [CP [TP someone [TP everyone [TP ⟨someone⟩) [likes ⟨everyone⟩]..]
(some > every)

The unambiguous scope relation in (9a) argues for vacuous movement to Spec,TP in subject *wh*-movement.

2.2.2 Anti-Agreement in Bantu

The second piece of evidence for (8) comes from agreement phenomena in Kinande, a Bantu language. In this language, as shown in (11), an anti-agreement marker *u*- will appear on the verb when the subject undergoes *wh*-movement; a canonical agreement marker *a*-, which is otherwise observed, is never possible in the movement. Consider the following examples:

(11) a. iyondi yo *a-/u-alangira   Marya?
         who   that AGR-/ANTI.AGR-saw Mary
         'Who saw Mary?'
     b. Kambale a-/*u-alangira   Marya.
         Kambale AGR-/ANTI.AGR-saw Mary
         'Kambale saw Mary.'
        (Schneider-Zioga 2007:404)

Under the current minimalist assumptions, ϕ-features are valued by Agree based on probe-goal relations. It is reasonable, then, to assume that the features are valued in the same way in both (11a) and (11b), and that ϕ-feature agreement is irrelevant to the agreement contrast. Building on the observation that agreement in Bantu always reflects Spec-Head (Kinyalolo 1991; see also Koopman 2006), I argue that Spec-Head effects on agreement (or canonical agreement) are reducible to the problem of externalization: that is, as illustrated in (12), movement to Spec,TP works as a syntactic instruction to the externalization component that agreement is realized canonically.

(12) *Spec-Head effects on agreement* (canonical agreement): Agree + IM with TP

$$[_{CP} \text{ C } [_{TP} n\text{P}_{\{\phi\}} [\text{T}_{\{\phi\}} [_{vP} \ldots \langle n\text{P}_{\{\phi\}} \rangle \ldots]..]$$

Morphological realization of ϕ-features (i.e., Spec-Head agreement) is not syntactic but a property of externalization, the locus of variation, under SMT. This argument is supported by examples in (13) and (14). These examples argue that verbal agreement is not full or is not canonically realized (hence, it is defective/default) when the subjects are post-verbal and do not move to Spec,TP.

(13) a. Wasal -a al- tullab -u.   *Standard Arabic*
arrived 3.M.SG the students NOM
'The students arrived.'
b. Al- tullab -u wasal -uu.
the students NOM arrived PL
(Ouhalla 1993:487, 514–515)

(14) a. E' vegnú qualche putela.   *Trentino*
is come some girls
'Some girls have come.'
b. *L'è vegnuda qualche putela. (full agreement)
they are come some girls
cf. c. La Maria la parla.
the Maria she speaks
'Maria speaks.' (full agreement)
(Brandi and Cordin 1989:121–122, 113)

With the assumption that the realization of agreement is reducible to the problem of externalization (= (12)), the fact that only anti-agreement is possible in (11a) argues for (8): unlike in (11b), movement of the subject *wh*-phrase does not apply to TP and no Spec,TP is created, with the result that agreement cannot be realized canonically on the verb and anti-agreement appears.[10]

---

[10] The same argument can apply to object movement in VP (e.g., past participle agreement in French): the agreement is observed only when the object moves to Spec,VP.

2.2.3 Agent Focus

Kaqchikel, a Mayan language of Guatemala, provides us with another piece of evidence for (8). In this language, subject movement shows an interesting asymmetry: A′/*wh*-movement of subjects of transitive clauses realizes Agent Focus (AF) on that verb's morphology; on the other hand, A-movement (raising) of such subjects does not. To see this, consider the following examples from Erlewine (2016):[11]

(15) a. Achike *x-ø-u-tëj   / x-ø-u-tj-ö   ri wäy?
         who   COM-B3.SG-A3.SG-eat / COM-B3.SG-eat-**AF** the tortilla
         'Who ate the tortilla?'

  b. Achike   n-ø-a-b′ij   rat [chin x-oj-tz′et-ö   /
     who   INC-B3.SG-A2.SG-think   2.SG that COM-B1.PL-see-**AF** /
     *x-oj-r-tz′ët   roj]?
     COM-B1.PL-A3.SG-see   1.PL
     'Who do you think saw us?'

cf. c. Iwïr   x-ø-u-tëj   ri wäy   ri a Juan.
       yesterday COM-B3.SG-A3.SG-eat the tortilla Juan
       'Yesterday Juan ate the tortilla.'

Erlewine (2014, 2016) argues that AF is due to the fact that a subject *wh*-phrase does not move to Spec,TP before moving to Spec,CP; the movement, according to Erlewine, would violate Spec-to-Spec anti-locality (= (16b)): movement of an SO from Spec,XP must cross maximal projection other than XP. Given Erlewine's argument, AF constitutes evidence that the subject moves in one-fell swoop to Spec,CP from its first-merged position without moving to Spec,TP (= (16a)). The distribution of AF is summarized in (16).

(16) a. [$_{CP}$ subject [C [$_{TP}$ [T [$_{v*P}$ ⟨subject⟩ ...]..]
                                                     AF morphology on the verb

  b. *[$_{CP}$ subject [C [$_{TP}$ ⟨subject⟩ [T [$_{v*P}$ ⟨subject⟩ ...]..]

  c. [$_{CP}$ C [$_{TP}$ subject [T [$_{v*P}$ ⟨subject⟩ ...]..]
                                                  no AF morphology on the verb

Recall that under simplest Merge, the derivation in (16b) is pos-

---

[11] Abbreviations in the gloss: A = Set A agreement, B = Set B agreement, COM = completive aspect, INC = incompletive aspect, ø = empty string. For details of Kaqchikel and AF, see Erlewine (2016).

sible but that as we discussed in section 2.1, such derivation will be ruled out independently at the interfaces, without assuming Spec-to-Spec anti-locality; (16a) follows for the reason that subject *wh*-movement to Spec,TP violates NTC. Although the details of our theoretical arguments are different, Erlewine's observation of Kaqchikel AF applies for us as well. To the extent that Erlewine's analysis of AF is correct, it argues that a subject *wh*-phrase moves in one-fell swoop to Spec,CP from its first-merged position, providing another piece of empirical evidence for (8).[12]

2.2.4 XP Merger with TP

The Vacuous Movement Hypothesis is endorsed by subject *wh*-movement in Yiddish as well. In this language, an XP can be merged with TP to form its Spec when the subject is *wh*-moved. Consider the following examples (cited from Diesing 1988, 1990, 2004):

(17) a. Ikh   veys   nit [$_{CP}$ ver [$_{TP}$ es   hot   gegesn a brukve]].
     I   know   not   who   EXPL has   eaten a turnip
     'I don't know who has eaten a turnip.'

b. Zi   iz   gekumen zen [$_{CP}$ ver [$_{TP}$ frier   vet   kontshen]].
    she has come   see   who   earlier would finish
    'She has come to see who would finish earlier.'

In (17), where *wh*-movement of the subject *ver* 'who' is executed, the exple-

---

[12] Erlewine's analysis of AF predicts that if A'-movement of transitive subjects does not violate Spec-to-Spec anti-locality, then AF will not appear on the verb even if the subjects undergo A'-movement. This prediction is borne out by (i), where the adverb *kanqtzij* 'actually' intervenes between the subject *wh*-phrase and the verb. In this case, AF is not allowed. Erlewine argues that Spec-to-Spec anti-locality can be evaded by the intervening adverb.

(i) Achike *kanqtzij* x-ø-u-tëj   / *x-ø-tj-ö   ri   wäy?
    who   actually   COM-B3.SG-A3.SG-eat / COM-B3.SG.-eat-**AF** the tortilla
    'Who actually ate the tortilla?'

I argue that in (i), the *wh*-phrase, as I have proposed, undergoes the derivation illustrated in (16a) but that the absence of AF is due to the fact that the adverb is merged with TP, which creates Spec,TP; we should note that cancellation of AF does not depend specifically on transitive subjects in the Spec of TP.

(ii) [$_{CP}$ subject [C [$_{TP}$ *kanqtzij* [T [$_{v*P}$ ⟨subject⟩ ...]..]   *no AF morphology on the verb*
    (→ (16c))

As we discuss immediately below as well as in section 4.2, merge of non-subjects with TP is in fact observed in other languages.

tive *es* and the adverb *frier* 'earlier' are merged in the subject position. As shown in (18), the same observation can be found in long-distance subject *wh*-movement from the embedded clause.

(18) a. ?Ver hot er moyre [$_{CP}$ az [$_{TP}$ es vet kumen]]?
 who has he fear that EXPL will come
 'Who does he fear will come?'
 b. ?Ver hot er moyre [$_{CP}$ az [$_{TP}$ haynt vet kumen]]?
 who has he fear that today will come
 'Who does he afraid will come?'

The Yiddish examples argue that a subject *wh*-phrase is not merged with TP. If the subject *wh*-phrase were moved to Spec,TP in (17) and (18), the so-called "EPP" would be satisfied, which will exclude further merge with TP. Under the simplest-Merge hypothesis, where Merge applies freely and the EPP or its equivalents do not exist (Mizuguchi 2014b), with the EPP effects, as I discuss immediately below, deducible from labeling, merge of the subject with TP or the λ-marked set will suffice for labeling through minimal search LA (Chomsky 2013, 2014a,b, 2015) and no further merge with the β-marked set will be required for Full Interpretation. Consider (19). As illustrated, merge of the subject *wh*-phrase with the λ-marked set will label the set as TP and β as <ϕ, ϕ>.[13, 14]

(19) a. [$_\beta$ *Wh*P$_{subj}$ [$_\lambda$ T$_{\{\phi\}}$ VP]] (β = <ϕ, ϕ>, λ = TP)
 b.

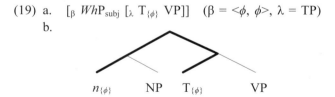

Further merge of an XP with the β-marked set is, in fact, allowed under the simplest-Merge hypothesis and will create multiple XP-YP structures as in (20).

(20) [$_\alpha$ XP [$_\beta$ *Wh*P$_{subj}$ [$_\lambda$ T$_{\{\phi\}}$ VP]]]

---

[13] Bold lines in (19) and elsewhere in this paper represent minimal search by LA. Tree notations like (19) are quite misleading. For our purpose here, we assume that a set and its familiar tree notation are equivalent.
[14] As I discuss in section 2.4, this SO will incur another interpretive problem at the CI interface.

This SO, however, will incur an interpretive problem for the creation of multiple XP-YP structures and will be ruled out at the CI interface. Notice that LA would label the α-marked set in (20) as XP through minimal search, not as TP. Consider (21).

(21) a. [α XP [β *Wh*P$_{subj}$ [λ T$_{\{\phi\}}$ VP]]]   (α = XP)
     b.

```
         α
        / \
       X   YP
          /  \
        n{ϕ}  \
             / \
           NP  T{ϕ}  VP
```

This has the effect that the intrinsic selectional relation between C and T will be violated at the CI interface for wrong labeling (Chomsky 2004, Fortuny 2008): C selects T but not X (X = n in (17a), (18a) and Adv in (17b), (18b)). The SO in (20)/(21a), though it can be produced by simplest Merge without any problems, will violate a CI interface condition at the relevant interface.

As I have discussed, if a subject *wh*-phrase is merged with TP, further merge of an XP will yield multiple XP-YP structures which would be labeled wrongly, ruled out at the CI interface. Notice that the same argument applies even if an XP is merged with the λ-marked set prior to a subject *wh*-phrase: minimal search LA would locate n of the set {n, NP} (the subject *wh*-phrase) as the label of α.[15]

(22) [α *Wh*P$_{subj}$ [β XP [λ T$_{\{\phi\}}$ VP]]]   (α = nP)

The selectional relation in question can only be satisfied in (17) and (18) if the subject *wh*-phrase does not move to Spec,TP and multiple XP-YP structures are not created. The Yiddish examples argue for the derivation in (8).

2.2.5 Quantifier Float in the Object Position

Finally, consider quantifier float in a West Ulster variety of English discussed in McCloskey (2000). In this variety, unlike in the standard variety, quantifi-

---

[15] Details of labeling of multiple XP-YP structures have to await further research, however, since there are languages which do allow such structures (e.g., Japanese). See also Narita and Fukui (2014) for multiple XP-YP.

ers like *all* can be stranded in the object position. As the following examples demonstrate, however, the stranding is well-formed only in *wh*-movement; it is not possible with subject raising:

(23) a. Who was arrested all in Duke St.?
     b. What was said all at the meeting?

(24) a. *They were arrested all last night.
     b. *They were spoken to all after class.
       (McCloskey 2000:72, 77)

How the above contrast is explained in a principled manner has to await further research. The contrast, however, is descriptively clear cut and provides us with at least observational evidence for the Vacuous Movement Hypothesis I have proposed. The examples do suggest that the subject behaves in different ways depending on whether it is a *wh*-phrase or not. Given that quantifier float in the object position is well-formed in (23), it can reasonably be concluded that the ill-formedness of (24) is not due to quantifier float in the object position. Considering that a normal subject is merged with TP and moves to its Spec, the well-formedness of quantifier float implies that the ill-formedness of (24) is reduced to subject movement to Spec,TP. Then if the subjects in (23) were merged in the same way, moving to the Spec of TP, just as those in (24), (23) would be no different in the syntax of subject movement. The well-formedness of (23), in contrast with the ill-formedness of (24), naturally follows if we assume that the subject does not behave uniformly in (23) and (24): that is, subject *wh*-phrases, unlike normal subjects, move vacuously to Spec,TP, undergoing the derivation in (8) (see also McCloskey 2000:77 for this argument based on the relevant data). We can say based on the descriptive contrast in (23) and (24) that quantifier float in West Ulster English speaks for (8).

2.2.6 Interim Summary
Summarizing the discussion thus far, I have considered five pieces of evidence for (8). As we have seen, the evidence bears out the derivation in which a subject *wh*-phrase is merged with CP and moves vacuously to the Spec of TP. We can conclude that empirical as well as theoretical arguments confirm the Vacuous Movement Hypothesis proposed in (8).

2.3 Subject-Initial Verb Second
The Vacuous Movement Hypothesis, which has been proposed for a subject

wh-phrase (or subject operators in general) under SMT, naturally extends to subject-initial Verb Second (V2) in Germanic languages. In this section, I argue that subject-initial V2 is also a straightforward consequence of simplest Merge.

For our purpose here, I discuss German as an example of V2 languages. It has been argued in the literature that V2 in German applies at the CP level and that when the subject is V2ed, it also moves to Spec,CP. The example in (25) is analyzed as (26a), instead of (26b), and subject-initial clauses are uniformly analyzed as V2 clauses (van Craenenbroeck and Haegeman 2007, Vikner 1995, Schwartz and Vikner 1986, 1996 among others).

(25) Die Kinder haben den Film gesehen.
 the children have the film seen
 'The children saw the film.'

(26) a. [$_{CP}$ Die Kinder [haben [$_{TP}$ T [$_{v*P}$ den Film gesehen]..]
 b. [$_{CP}$ C [$_{TP}$ Die Kinder [haben [$_{v*P}$ den Film gesehen]..]

One argument for (26a) is that TP-adjoined adverbs like *gestern* 'yesterday' and *letzte Woche* 'last week', which cannot adjoin to modify non-subject initial V2 clauses, cannot adjoin to subject-initial V2 clauses, either. Consider the following examples:

(27) a. *Gestern diese Sache hat Peter erledigt.
 yesterday this matter has Peter taken-care-of
 'Yesterday, Peter took care of this matter.'
 b. *Letzte Woche ein Buch hat Peter tatsächlich gelesen.
 last week a book has Peter actually read
 'Last week Peter actually read a book.'

(28) a. *Gestern Peter hat diese Sache erledigt.
 b. *Letzte Woche Peter hat tatsächlich ein Buch gelesen.

If subject-initial clauses are CPs, with the subject in Spec,CP, then the ill-formedness of (28) can be explained on par with that of (27).

Likewise, if the analysis in (26a) is correct, then it predicts that the adverbs in question can come between *hat* and *diese Sache/tatsächlich* because the former is supposed to be in CP and the latter in TP. This prediction is, indeed, confirmed by the following examples:

(29) a. Peter hat *gestern* diese Sache erledigt.
 b. Peter hat *letzte Woche* tatsächlich ein Buch gelesen.

The examples above argue that the subject is outside TP and hence, is merged in CP.

Another argument is that A'-movement out of embedded subject-initial clauses is as ill-formed as A'-movement from embedded V2 clauses. Consider (30) and (31).[16]

(30) *Welchen Film hat sie gesagt, [die Kinder] haben gesehen?
　　　which　　film　has　she　said　　the children　have　seen
　　　'Which film did she say the children saw?'

(31) *Welchen Film hat sie gesagt, [in der Schule] haben die Kinder gesehen?
　　　which　　film　has　she　said　　in the school　have　the children
　　　seen
　　　'Which film did she say the children saw in the school?'

(31) shows that movement out of the embedded CP is prevented if an XP (here, *in der Schule*) is V2ed in the embedded clause; an element in the Spec of the embedded CP blocks A'-movement out of the clause. As we can see from (30), movement out of the subject-initial embedded clause is also ill-formed, which reasonably argues that the subject in subject-initial clauses is V2ed and moves to Spec,CP.

The two arguments above and others discussed in the references cited above demonstrate that in subject-initial clauses, the subject is in Spec,CP. I argue that vacuous movement proposed for operator subjects can also apply to subject-initial V2: just like operator subjects, the subject is merged with CP (the root) at the phase level and moves vacuously to Spec,TP in subject-initial clauses. Subject-initial V2 constitutes another example in which the subject undergoes the derivation in (8).

2.4 Simultaneous Movement

I have argued that the subject is merged only with CP and moves vacuously to Spec,TP when it undergoes A'-movement. In this section, I discuss simultaneous movement of a subject *wh*-phrase, arguing that the derivation will produce an SO which will cause interpretive and externalization problems.

Chomsky (2007, 2008) argues in the phase-based system of syntax that in subject *wh*-movement, a subject *wh*-phrase moves simultaneously at the

---

[16] In German, V2 is allowed in the embedded clause when *daß* 'that' is not present in C. See examples (55) in section 4.1.

phase level to the Specs of CP and TP from its first-merged position. The proposed derivation is illustrated in (32).

(32) [$_{CP}$ which student$_i$ [C [$_{TP}$ which student$_j$ [T [$_{v*P}$ ⟨which student$_{i,\,j}$⟩
[v^*-read the book]..]

In (32), the subject *wh*-phrase does not move from Spec,TP to Spec,CP and the problems we have noted in section 2.1 as well as in footnote 5 do not arise here.

Simultaneous movement, though it could be possible in principle under simplest Merge, will raise other problems. In (32), there is no direct relation between *which student$_i$* and *which student$_j$*, each of which forms a distinct chain and is a head of that chain. To put it differently, two independent chains are produced in (32) by the simultaneous IM at the phase level, just as distinct chains are yielded in (33) by IM of *John* and *what*; in (33), the subject and the object are not in a chain relation and form distinct chains by their movements.

(33) a. What did John read?
 b. [$_{CP}$ what$_i$ [C [$_{TP}$ John$_j$ [T [$_{v*P}$ ⟨what$_i$⟩ [⟨John$_j$⟩ [v^*-read ⟨what$_i$⟩]..]

Then as in (33), in (32), each of the two chains yielded by simultaneous movement of the subject (that is, (*which student$_j$, which student$_j$*) and (*which student$_i$, which student$_i$*)) will be subject to both semantic interpretation and the rules of externalization. The chain created by *which student* in the Spec of TP will incur an interpretive problem at the CI interface: the subject, the head of the (*which student$_j$, which student$_j$*) chain, is not in the right position where it can form an operator-variable relation with its copy, and the chain cannot be interpreted properly at the CI interface. As evidenced by (34a), which is analyzed as (34b), a single operator, if it does not move to Spec,CP, will not be able to receive proper interpretation in English, causing interpretive ill-formedness.[17]

(34) a. *Did you read what? (intended: What did you read?)
 b. [$_{CP}$ Did [you [$_{v*P}$ v^*-read [$_{VP}$ what [$_\kappa$ V ⟨what⟩]..]

As a result, the derived SO in (32) would be ruled out at the CI interface.

---

[17] I assume that the object moves to Spec,VP; otherwise, the κ-marked set in (34b) will not be labeled and a labeling failure will arise (Chomsky 2014a,b, 2015).

Furthermore, simultaneous movement anticipates that the head of each chain (*which student* in Spec,CP and the one in Spec,TP) will be externalized. (33) argues that each chain head is, in fact, pronounced. As (35) demonstrates, however, the externalization of *which student*$_i$ and *which student*$_j$ will result in anomaly and is not empirically borne out (see also footnote 4).

(35) *Which student which student read the book?

The two arguments above persuasively indicate that the subject *wh*-phrase does not head a chain in Spec,TP and that simultaneous movement does not take place. Notice that the problems we have noted do not arise under the Vacuous Movement Hypothesis: Merge applies only to CP and only a single chain is created by the merge of the subject *which student*.[18, 19]

2.5 Summary

In this section, I have proposed (8) as the derivation of subject *wh*-movement, arguing that the Vacuous Movement Hypothesis is deduced from simplest Merge. As we have discussed, the proposed analysis based on theoretical arguments is empirically borne out. I also argued that the proposed analysis can straightforwardly extend to subject-initial V2 in Germanic languages and can evade the interpretive and externalization problems raised by simultaneous movement of a subject *wh*-phrase.

3 Labeling of "TP"

3.1 A-Properties of the Subject and the Problem of EPP

In the discussion thus far, I have maintained that under simplest Merge, a subject *wh*-phrase (more generally, an operator subject) is merged only with CP, moving vacuously to the Spec of TP. This proposal, however, may raise problems if we consider the fact that a subject *wh*-phrase shows properties of A-movement. As we can see from (36), subject *wh*-phrases, like normal subjects in (37), can bind a reflexive and do not cause weak crossover violations.

(36) a.   *Who* seems to *himself* to be intelligent?

---

[18] This conclusion will reject Huybregts's (2005) analysis of *that-t* effects, which crucially relies on simultaneous, parallel movement. I discuss *that-t* effects in section 4.

[19] We should note that the same problems will arise when a subject *wh*-phrase moves to Spec,CP and Spec,TP one by one at the phase level.

b. *Who* seems to *his* professor to be hard-working?

(37) a. *John* seems to *himself* to be intelligent.
b. *Every student* seems to *his* professor to be hard-working.

Spec,CP, in which the subjects in (36) are merged, is considered an A'-position, however. As evidenced by (38), an object *wh*-phrase cannot bind a reflexive in Spec,CP and its movement to the relevant Spec position incurs weak crossover violations.

(38) a. **Which students* did *each other*'s teachers criticize?
b. **Who* does *his* mother love?

If Spec,CP is an A'-position, then the question arises: How can a subject *wh*-phrase come to bear A-properties in Spec,CP if, as I proposed, it does not move to Spec,TP and moves only to Spec,CP?

I submit that the answer lies in head movement, arguing that A-properties of a subject *wh*-phrase come from T-to-C movement. I assume that head movement is implemented in narrow syntax for the reason that it shows syntactic properties and has clear effects on semantic interpretation (see, e.g., Mathew 2015, Ogawa 2008 and Roberts 2010b). In Minimalism, movement is considered (Internal) Merge. Head movement, if it is a form of Merge, clearly violates NTC because it applies counter-cyclically and is pair-merged to another head already merged in the derivation, which does tamper with structures already created. I argue that head movement is not a form of Merge. Instead, I propose that it is an upward counterpart to feature inheritance: that is, head movement is nothing other than "feature climbing" from lower heads (or non-phase heads) to higher heads (or phase heads); the latter "inherits" featural properties from the former. Notice that feature climbing (upward feature inheritance), just like downward feature inheritance, does not violate NTC.[20]

(39) Head Movement = "Feature Climbing"
$[Z\ [Y_{\{\chi\}}\ [_{XP}\ ...]..] \rightarrow [Z_{\{\chi\}}\ [Y\ [_{XP}\ ...]..]$
(where Z is a higher head; Y a lower head)

Feature climbing should be possible as far as syntax is free, with features going upwards as well as downwards; only a stipulation can block upward

---

[20] See Chomsky (2015), Narita (2014), Narita and Fukui (2014) for other approaches to head movement in SMT-based Minimalism.

feature inheritance. Thanks to head movement qua feature climbing, C acquires featural properties from T without violating NTC and a subject *wh*-phrase can bear A-properties in the Spec of CP; head movement renders Spec,CP an A-position. Since C still retains its own properties, the subject can bear A'-properties as well. Consequently, the occurrences of the subject can be interpreted properly at the CI interface by forming an operator-variable chain; also, LA can label the set $\{\{nP_{subj}\}, \{CP\}\}$ without any problems by minimal detection of agreeing heads ($n_{\{Q\}}$, $C_{\{Q\}}$).

The proposed approach to head movement can not only explain A-properties of the subject in Spec,CP; it can also solve the problem of EPP, which is now considered a labeling problem. Chomsky (2013, 2014a,b, 2015) argues that subject EPP effects are forced by labeling of the λ-marked set as well as labeling of the α-marked set (an XP-YP structure). Consider (40).

(40) [C [$_λ$ T$_{\{\phi\}}$ [$_α$ nP [$_{v*P}$ v*-read the book]..]   (λ = unlabeled)

In English-type languages, unlike in Italian-type languages, T$_{\{\phi\}}$, like a root, is too weak to serve as a label. Then in (40), the λ-marked set will be left unlabeled. However, if an SO (most typically, an nP) is merged with the λ-marked set and an XP-YP structure is formed as in (41b), T is strengthened as a label with the help of the SO and can label the set.

(41) a. [C [$_λ$ T$_{\{\phi\}}$ [$_α$ SO$_{\{\phi\}}$ [$_{v*P}$ v*-read the book]..]
   b. [C [$_γ$ SO$_{\{\phi\}}$ [$_λ$ T$_{\{\phi\}}$ [$_α$ ⟨SO$_{\{\phi\}}$⟩ [$_{v*P}$ v*-read the book]..]
                                         (λ = TP; γ = <ϕ, ϕ>)

As shown, subject EPP effects are deducible from labeling of λ as well as labeling of α. In the Vacuous Movement Hypothesis proposed in (8), however, notice that an nP is not at all merged with the λ-marked set; if T$_{\{\phi\}}$ cannot serve as a label for its weakness, then the λ-marked set would be unlabeled, which would violate Full Interpretation.

I argue that head movement qua feature climbing can give a solution to the problem at hand. Featural properties of T, including its ϕ-features, climb onto C thanks to head movement, which has the effect that it gets on par with raising T: that is, T without ϕ-features. As evidenced by (42), raising T, unlike T$_{\{\phi\}}$, can stand even without merge of an nP with the λ-marked set, which suggests that it can indeed serve as a label and that the λ-marked set can be labeled as TP in (42) (Epstein, Kitahara, and Seely 2014, Goto 2013).

(42) a. There seems/is likely [$_λ$ to [be a man in the room]].   (λ = TP)

b. The man seems/is likely [$_\lambda$ to [be ⟨a man⟩ in the room]].

$$(\lambda = TP)$$

Thanks to feature climbing, the λ-marked set in (43) (= (8)), just like that in (42), can be successfully labeled even without merge of an operator subject (nP_{subj}) with the relevant set.

(43) [$_\delta$ nP_{subj} [$_\epsilon$ C$_{\{\phi\}}$ [$_\lambda$ T [$_\alpha$ ⟨nP_{subj}⟩ [$_{v*P}$ v^* [$_{VP}$ ...]..]   (λ = TP)

A labeling problem does not arise and the absence of EPP follows.[21]

To summarize this section, I proposed that A-properties of a subject *wh*-phrase merged in Spec,CP are warranted by head movement. I argued that head movement is "feature climbing," which is an upward counterpart to feature inheritance. I also demonstrated that it can also solve the problem of labeling of "TP" (that is, the λ-marked set in (43)) in subject *wh*-movement, showing that subject EPP effects are deducible from labeling.

3.2 Head Movement and Lack of EPP

If head movement qua feature climbing can render T$_{\{\phi\}}$ on par with raising T, enabling it to label, optionality of EPP follows. In this section, I discuss two empirical cases which endorse this argument.

The first case is found in the expletive construction in Icelandic. The following examples show that in passive and unaccusative expletive constructions, there are two positions in a clause where a passive/unaccusative subject can surface (the subjects in (44) and (45) are typed in bold).

(44) a.   Það   hafa   **margir   bílar**   verið   seldir   á   þessu   uppboði.
          there have   many   cars   been   sold   at   this   auction
          'Many cars have been sold at this auction.'
     b.   Það hafa verið seldir **margir bílar** á þessu uppboði.
cf. c.   **Margir bílar** hafa verið seldir á þessu uppboði.
          (Jonas 1996:11)

(45) a.   Það   hafa   **margir   menn**   komið   hingað   í dag.
          there have   many   men   come   here   today
          'Many men have come here today.'

---

[21] In (43), syntactically valued ϕ-features are located in C, a phase head, through feature climbing. This does not cause any problems if unvalued features remain uninterpretable even if they are valued, and are simply invisible to the CI interface (Epstein, Kitahara, and Seely 2010).

b. Það hafa komið **margir menn** hingað í dag.
(Koeneman and Neeleman 2001:207)

As we discuss in section 4.2.4, *það* 'there' in Icelandic is available only in V2 contexts and is merged in Spec,CP when nothing is moved to this Spec. With this background in mind, it can reasonably be said that the subject occupies Spec,TP in (44a) and (45a) because it comes between CP and *v*P. The fact that (44b) and (45b) are also possible then suggests that Spec,TP (or EPP in T) is optional in Icelandic. This optionality of EPP is straightforward under our proposal. In Icelandic V2, the verb, along with T, head-moves all the way up to C. If head movement is feature climbing, this means that featural properties of T climb onto C, with the result that the λ-marked set can be labeled for lack of ϕ-features in T. Whether the subject moves to Spec,TP or not, which is freely available under simplest Merge, labeling of the λ-marked set can be executed thanks to head movement and the derivation converges at the interfaces.[22]

The other case of optionality of EPP which can be deduced from labeling via feature climbing is found in Yiddish. As the following examples demonstrate, in this language, the subject or the expletive *es* has to be merged with the λ-marked set in the embedded clause:

(46) a. Vos hot er nit gevolt [$_{CP}$ az [$_\gamma$ mir [$_\lambda$ zoln
what has he not wanted that we should
[leyenen ⟨vos⟩]..]?
read
'What did he not want us to read?'
b. ?Vos hot er nit gevolt [$_{CP}$ az [$_\gamma$ es [$_\lambda$ zoln [mir leyenen ⟨vos⟩]..]?
(Diesing 1990:71–72)

This is a well-known EPP effect, which, as we have discussed in 3.1, can be given a principled explanation by labeling: T is strengthened and qualified as a label by Spec,TP (see (41)).

It is interesting to observe that merge of the subject/the expletive does not occur when T moves to C. Consider the following examples (Diesing

---

[22] Some may wonder how the λ-marked set is labeled in (44a) and (45a), where the subject *n*P is merged with that set; if ϕ-features climb onto C, then the λ-marked set will not be labeled for the reason that agreeing heads cannot be detected by LA through minimal search (Epstein, Kitahara, and Seely 2014 for relevant discussion). I assume that in the relevant examples, all the features except ϕ-features climb onto C.

ibid.):[23]

(47) a. Vos hot er nit gevolt [$_{CP}$ zoln-C [$_\lambda$ ⟨zoln⟩ [$_{v*P}$ mir leyenen ⟨vos⟩]]]?
   b. *Vos hot er nit gevolt [$_{CP}$ az [$_\lambda$ zoln [$_{v*P}$ mir leyenen ⟨vos⟩]]]?

The examples above argue that Yiddish shows optionality of EPP when T undergoes head movement. Our proposal can straightforwardly explain this optionality: the head movement, which is nothing other than feature climbing from T to C, can deprive ϕ-features of T and consequently, T can serve as a label and the λ-marked can be successfully labeled as TP. Labeling of λ can be executed without merging an nP with the λ-marked set. On the other hand, (47b) is ill-formed for a labeling failure: T-to-C head movement is blocked by the overt complementizer (see section 4) and ϕ-features are stuck in T, with the result that labeling of the λ-marked set will fail unless an nP is merged with that set as in (46). The derived SO, when transferred, cannot be interpreted or externalized, ruled out at the interfaces.

I have demonstrated with two empirical examples that optionality of EPP is deducible from labeling through feature climbing. In fact, this proposal can deduce the well-known generalization that V2 languages have optionality of the subject in Spec,TP: in such languages, feature climbing (T-to-C head movement) takes place for V2 and the λ-marked set can be labeled as TP, which allows the subject not to be merged with the relevant set (informally, TP) for the labeling.

3.3 Subject Topicalization

The proposed analysis of EPP in terms of labeling (Full Interpretation) can also explain the behaviors of subject topicalization. First, consider local subject topicalization. As (48) shows, local subject topicalization is prohibited (Lasnik and Saito 1992).

(48) a. *The man, read the book.
   b. *I think that the man, read the book.

I argue that the ill-formedness of (48) is reducible to a labeling failure. Consider the derivation of (48). In the derivational process, the topic subject

---

[23] In (47a), it looks as if *zoln* 'should' moves to C from T, which is for expository purposes only. Recall that head movement is feature climbing and there is no head movement in the traditional sense; phonological effects of head movement or feature climbing come out through externalization.

the man, which is an operator just like a *wh*-phrase, is merged with CP or TopP in the left periphery, undergoing vacuous movement to Spec,TP. Since an *n*P is not merged with the λ-marked set, the labeling of the relevant set will be possible when head movement takes place and ϕ-features move out of T. However, in topicalization, unlike in *wh*-movement, head movement does not take place. Consider (49).

(49) a. *The Minimalist Program, did John read carefully.
b. *I think that the Minimalist Program, should John read carefully.

Under our proposal, this is to say that ϕ-features in T do not climb onto C in topicalization. If head movement is not implemented, then ϕ-features will remain in T, with the result that the λ-marked set will be left unlabeled for the weakness of $T_{\{\phi\}}$ as a label.

(50) [$_\delta$ the man [$_\varepsilon$ C$_{\{Topic\}}$ [$_\lambda$ T$_{\{\phi\}}$ [$_\alpha$ ⟨the man⟩ [$_{v*P}$ v^* [$_{VP}$ ...]..]

(λ = unlabeled)

Taking into account the independently motivated assumption that head movement (that is, feature climbing) does not occur in topicalization, the ban on local subject topicalization can be deduced from a labeling failure, hence the violation of Full Interpretation.[24]

Interestingly enough, long-distance subject topicalization is well-formed.

---

[24] Recall that in German subject-initial V2, the subject is merged with CP just as in topicalization. Subject-initial V2 does not incur a labeling failure because head movement to C is executed in German V2 and ϕ-features climb out of T, with the result that T can serve as a label.

In Japanese, local subject topicalization is possible. Consider (i).

(i) Taroo-wa kinoo LGB-o yon-da.
Taroo-TOP yesterday LGB-ACC read-PAST
'Taroo read LGB yesterday.'

In Japanese, a subject marked with *-wa* is a topic and is topicalized. Following Kuroda (1992), suppose that the *wa*-marked subject, unlike a subject marked with *-ga*, is in Spec,CP. If so, the subject is merged with CP, undergoing vacuous movement to Spec,TP under our proposal. The well-formedness of (i), in contrast with the ill-formedness of English (48), is attributable to the fact that Japanese $T_{\{\phi\}}$, unlike that in English, is strong enough to serve as a label and the λ-marked set can be labeled even without ϕ-feature climbing, which also explains the absence of *that-t* effects in Japanese. For this discussion, see section 4.2.1 and footnote 29.

Consider (51).[25]

(51) a. John, I think left.
(Lasnik and Saito 1992:110)
b. The man, I think John said had left.

As far as the argument is correct that EPP is reducible to labeling, feature climbing can be executed in long-distance topicalization and the λ-marked set can be labeled in (51). I maintain that this is indeed the case in the embedded clause. The key component of the well-formedness of (51) is successive-cyclic movement of the subject. In the derivation of (51), the operator subject undergoes trans-phasal movement by way of phasal Specs. Hence, it is moved to the Spec of the embedded CP in the course of the derivation. I argue that successive-cyclic movement to the embedded Spec,CP allows feature climbing to C; in other words, such movement triggers head movement. The evidence can be found in Belfast English, where, as the following examples illustrate, successive-cyclic *wh*-movement induces subject-auxiliary inversion, hence head movement, in the path of the movement:

(52) a. Who did John hope would he see?
b. What did Mary claim did they steal?
c. I wonder what did John think would he get.
(Henry 1995:108)

Considering that *wh*-phrases move through the highest Specs in the CP domain for trans-phasal movement, these examples suggest that movement to these Specs (successive-cyclic movement through phasal Specs) makes head movement or feature climbing possible, which is simply not externalized in Standard English. Provided that long-distance topicalization is an instance of trans-phasal movement, a topic subject will move in the same way, by way of the highest Specs (that is, Spec,CP) and feature climbing can obtain in the embedded clause thanks to successive-cyclic movement of the subject to phasal Spec,CP in the course of the derivation. Thus in (51), the λ-marked set can be labeled through ϕ-feature climbing to C and the topicalization is ruled in as well-formed at the interfaces.

---

[25] The ill-formedness of (i) is a well-known *that-t* effect, which I discuss in section 4.

(i) a. *John, I think that left.
b. *The man, I think John said that had left.

4 ECP Effects on Subject *Wh*-Movement

In the discussion thus far, we have considered the syntax of subject *wh*/A′-movement. Under the assumptions of SMT, I have argued for the Vacuous Movement Hypothesis for operator subjects (one instance of which is a subject *wh*-phrase) (= (8)), showing that vacuous movement to Spec,TP, coupled with feature climbing (head movement), can derive the absence of EPP effects on the subject in terms of labeling. In this section, I submit that the proposed analysis can deduce ECP effects on subject *wh*-movement, showing that the effects are reducible to violations of Full Interpretation at the interfaces.

4.1 ECP as a Labeling Failure
ECP effects on the subject are typically observed in long-distance subject *wh*-movement. Consider the following examples:

(53) a. *Which student$_i$ does John think [that t$_i$ read the book]?
 b. Which book$_i$ does John think [that the student read t$_i$]?

In the Government and Binding framework, the overt complementizer in the embedded clause disallows antecedent government of the subject trace and causes an ECP (that is, *that-t*) violation in (53a); on the other hand, the trace of the object can be lexically governed even when *that* is present, thanks to which no ECP violation results in (53b). ECP can nicely explain the subject-object contrast in (53); however, it is still a descriptive generalization that needs a principled explanation. I propose that labeling deduces *that-t* effects: that is, ECP is reducible to labeling and hence, to the interface properties.

Consider the derivation of (53a). Long-distance *wh*-movement, which is an instance of trans-phasal movement, undergoes successive-cyclic movement to phasal Specs for cyclic Transfer in the course of the derivation. In the relevant derivation, the subject *wh*-phrase thus moves to the Spec of the embedded CP. In the embedded CP phase, as in the root, the subject is merged with CP in a way satisfying NTC, moving to its Spec and undergoing vacuous movement to Spec,TP (see also Rizzi 2006, 2014, Rizzi and Shlonskey 2007). This derivation is empirically supported by Kaqchikel (15b). Recall that in (15b), the embedded verb shows AF in long-distance subject *wh*-movement, just as the verb does in local subject *wh*-movement (= (15a)), which indicates that the subject, as we have argued, does not move to the embedded Spec,TP. The examples are repeated below for convenience.

SIMPLEST MERGE, LABELING, AND A'-MOVEMENT OF THE SUBJECT   67

(15) a. Achike *x-ø-u-tëj   / x-ø-u-tj-ö   ri wäy?
         who   COM-B3.SG-A3.SG-eat / COM-B3.SG-eat-AF the tortilla
         'Who ate the tortilla?'
    b.   Achike n-ø-a-b'ij   rat [chin x-oj-tz'et-ö   /
         who   INC-B3.SG-A2.SG-think   2.SG that COM-B1.PL-see-AF /
         *x-oj-r-tz'ët   roj]?
         COM-B1.PL-A3.SG-see 1.PL
         'Who do you think saw us?'

Simplest Merge yields (54b) from (54a).

(54) a. [$_{CP}$ that-C [$_\lambda$ T$_{\{\phi\}}$ [$_\alpha$ which student [$_{v*P}$ v*-read the book]..]
     b. [$_\delta$ which student$_i$ [$_{CP}$ that-C [$_\lambda$ T$_{\{\phi\}}$ [$_\alpha$ t$_i$ [$_{v*P}$ v*-read the book]..]

Recall that T$_{\{\phi\}}$ in English is too weak to serve as a label and that it can label when head movement or feature climbing of ϕ-features takes place and it gets on par with raising T; otherwise, the λ-marked set would not be labeled and would not be interpreted or externalized, which will violate Full Interpretation at the interfaces. In (54b), however, head movement qua feature climbing will fail. It has been observed that overt complementizers block head movement. Consider the following examples from German (55) and Belfast English (56) (see also (47b)):

(55) a. Er sagt, daß die Kinder   diesen Film gesehen haben.
         he says that the children this   film seen   have
         'He says that the children saw this film.'
    b.   *Er sagt, daß die Kinder haben diesen Film gesehen.
    c.   Er sagt, die Kinder haben diesen Film gesehen.
         (Vikner 1995:66)

(56) a. *Who did John hope that could he help?
    b.   Who did John hope that he could help?
         (Henry 1995:109)

In (55), when *daß* 'that' is present in the embedded clause, *haben* 'have' cannot move and V2, which is available when there is no overt complementizer, is not possible in the embedded clause. Likewise, in Belfast English, where successive-cyclic movement triggers head movement (recall (52)), the overt complementizer blocks otherwise possible subject-auxiliary inversion in the embedded clause.

A reasonable assumption drawn from (55) and (56) under the proposed analysis of head movement is that overt complementizers cannot function as receptacles for transmitted features. For our purpose, suppose that phonological features borne by overt lexical items in higher heads prevent feature climbing from lower heads. Then in (54b), ϕ-features will get stuck in the embedded T, with the result that the λ-marked set will be left unlabeled for the weakness of ϕ-bearing T as a label in English. I claim that long-distance subject *wh*-movement out of the embedded clause with an overt complementizer will cause a labeling failure of the λ-marked set, with ECP or *that-t* effects reducible to violations of Full Interpretation.

(57)   [$_\delta$ *wh*P$_{subj}$ [that-C [$_\lambda$ T$_{\{\phi\}}$ [$_\alpha$ ⟨*wh*P$_{subj}$⟩ [$_{v*P}$ *v** [$_{VP}$ ...]..]   (λ = unlabeled)

ϕ-*feature climbing*

A labeling failure of the λ-marked set deduces the ill-formedness of long-distance subject *wh*-movement out of the *that*-clause (= (53a)).[26]

On the other hand, if the complementizer is not overt, C can indeed serve as a receptacle for transmitted features and climbing of ϕ-features from T can be implemented without any problems (see (55c) and (52)). Thus, in (58), unlike in (53a), the λ-marked set can be labeled as TP, which satisfies Full Interpretation and the derivation is ruled in as well-formed at the interfaces.

(58)   Which student$_i$ does John think [$_\delta$ t$_i$ [C$_{\{\phi\}}$ [$_\lambda$ T [$_\alpha$ t$_i$ read the book]..]?
                                                                                     (λ = TP)

Furthermore, the proposed analysis straightforwardly explains why *that* is irrelevant in the case of long-distance object *wh*-movement out of the embedded clause: thanks to the IM of the subject, the λ-marked set can be labeled as TP (see section 3.1); labeling of λ can occur without feature climbing in the relevant case.

(59)   Which book$_i$ does John think [(that) the student read t$_i$]?

(60)   [$_\delta$ *wh*P$_{obj}$ [that-C [$_\gamma$ *n*P$_{subj}$ [$_\lambda$ T$_{\{\phi\}}$ [$_\alpha$ ⟨*wh*P$_{obj}$⟩ [⟨*n*P$_{subj}$⟩ [$_{v*P}$ *v** [$_{VP}$ ... ⟨*wh*P$_{obj}$⟩]..]   (λ = TP)

The subject-object contrast nicely follows from labeling (i.e., Full Interpretation at the interfaces).

---

[26] For much related discussion, see Chomsky (2014a,b, 2015). Mizuguchi (2008) proposes that *that-t* effects are reducible to EPP, which now follows from labeling. See also Rizzi (2006, 2014), who argues that ECP and EPP are unified by Criterial Freezing.

4.2 Labeling of λ and That-t *Effects*

I have argued that *that-t* effects are reducible to a labeling failure. Then the proposed labeling analysis makes the following prediction: if the λ-marked set in (57) can somehow be labeled, long-distance subject *wh*-movement will not show *that-t* effects even when the overt complementizer is present in the embedded clause and climbing of ϕ-features is blocked. In this section, I demonstrate that this prediction is borne out, arguing that the proposed analysis is empirically upheld.

4.2.1 Labelable T

First, Perlmutter (1971) and particularly, Rizzi (1982) note that *that-t* effects are not observed in null-subject languages. Consider the following examples:

(61) Chi credi [che ⟨chi⟩ verrà]?   *Italian*
 who think-you that will-come
 'Who do you think will come?'
 (Rizzi 1982:117)

(62) ¿Quién dijiste [que ⟨quién⟩ salió temprano]?   *Spanish*
 who said-you that left early
 'Who did you say left early?'
 (Perlmutter 1971:103)

(63) Pjos ipes [oti ⟨pjos⟩ egrapse afto to vivlio]?   *Greek*
 who said-2SG that wrote this the book
 'Who did you say wrote this book?'
 (Roberts and Holmberg 2010:17)

The following examples show that these languages allow empty or zero subjects:

(64) Compra un libro.   *Italian*
 buy-3SG a book
 'He/she buys a book.'

(65) Hemos trabajado todo el día.   *Spanish*
 have worked all the day
 'We have worked all day.'
 (Perlmutter *ibid.*)

(66) Mila ellinika.   *Greek*
 speaks Greek

'He/she speaks Greek.'
(Roberts and Holmberg *ibid.*)

Null-subject languages suggest that EPP can be optional, with no need to merge an *n*P with TP. Under the current Minimalist assumptions, where EPP follows from labeling, this is to say that the λ-marked set can be labeled even without the help of an *n*P: that is, $T_{\{\phi\}}$ in null-subject languages, unlike that in English, is strong enough to label (Chomsky 2014a,b, 2015). Consequently, the λ-marked set can be labeled as TP by LA without any problems through minimal detection of $T_{\{\phi\}}$.

(67) $[_\delta \ wh\text{P}_{\text{subj}} \ [\text{that-C} \ [_\lambda \ T_{\{\phi\}} \ [_\alpha \ \langle wh\text{P}_{\text{subj}}\rangle \ [_{v*\text{P}} \ ...]..] \quad (\lambda = \text{TP})$

A labeling failure does not occur with the λ-marked set in null-subject languages and as predicted, *that-t* effects are not observed even when feature-climbing of ϕ-features is blocked by overt complementizers.[27]

The next question that should be answered is where the parametric difference between labelable $T_{\{\phi\}}$ and unlabelable $T_{\{\phi\}}$ comes from. It has been noted that null subjects are attributed to "richness of agreement" (Rizzi 1982, Chomsky 2014a,b, 2015; see also Alexiadou and Anagnostopoulou 1998 and references cited therein). Under current assumptions, rich agreement makes $T_{\{\phi\}}$ strong enough to serve as a label, which I argue is reducible to the fact that subject agreement has historically developed from subject/demonstrative pronouns (van Gelderen 2011, Givón 1976, Roberts 2010a; see also Simpson and Wu 2001 for much related discussion). For instance, van Gelderen (2011) argues that agreement comes from a series of changes, which she calls the "subject agreement cycle" or "subject cycle," demonstrating the process of this change as (68).

---

[27] In the (southern) varieties of German where object extraction is fully acceptable from the embedded clause, subject extraction is possible from the embedded *daß* clause, showing no *that-t* effects (Rizzi 1990:119).

(i) Wer glaubst du, $[_{\text{CP}}$ daß [oft   nach Paris fährt]]?
     who think   you   that   often to   Paris goes
     'Who do you think often goes to Paris?'
     (Vikner 1995:13)

Lack of *that-t* effects in the relevant German dialects is explained in the same way if we take into account the fact that EPP is optional in German (Diesing 1992), which suggests that German $T_{\{\phi\}}$, like $T_{\{\phi\}}$ in null-subject languages, is labelable.

(68) a. demonstrative > third person pronoun > clitic > agreement > zero
b. noun/oblique/emphatic > first/second person pronoun > clitic > agreement > zero
(van Gelderen 2011:38)

With this background in place, I submit that in null-subject languages, the properties of pronouns, which have been reanalyzed, are still present in rich agreement, thanks to which such agreement can strengthen $T_{\{\phi\}}$ for labeling just as an $nP_{\{\phi\}}$ does; on the other hand, in non-null-subject languages, they have deteriorated and agreement has lost the properties of pronouns, hence poor agreement, due to which an nP is required in order for $T_{\{\phi\}}$ to label. Notice, however, that in both labelable $T_{\{\phi\}}$ and unlabelable $T_{\{\phi\}}$ languages, $T_{\{\phi\}}$ is strengthened to serve as a label in the same way, either by its internal properties of subject/demonstrative pronouns now reanalyzed as rich agreement (= (69a)) or by external properties of an nP (= (69b)).[28, 29]

(69)

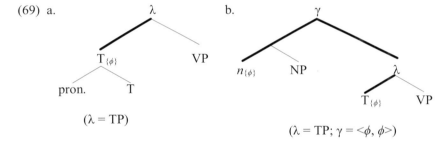

---

[28] The properties of subject/demonstrative pronouns, now reanalyzed as rich agreement, can also solve the problems of ϕ valuation and theta-role assignment.

[29] If richness of agreement makes $T_{\{\phi\}}$ strong enough to serve as a label, which allows null subjects, then it suggests that unlike the standard assumption, Japanese is a rich-agreement language. As the following examples illustrate, Japanese allows null subjects and as expected, *that*-t effects are not observed in long-distance subject movement (see also Abe 2015a, Ishii 2004):

(i) Sono hon-o yon-da.
the book-ACC read-PAST
'pro read the book.'

(ii) Dare-ga John-wa [_CP ⟨dare-ga⟩ sono hon-o yon-da to] omotteiru no?
who-NOM John-TOP the book-ACC read-PAST that think Q
'Who does John think read the book?'

I assume that Japanese has rich agreement lexically but that it is simply not externalized for lack of morphology. Further research will be left for future.

4.2.2 Merge of an XP$_{\{\phi\}}$

Secondly, there are languages where *that-t* effects are circumvented when XPs are merged in the derivation. Consider the following examples from Yiddish, Danish and Swedish, where merge of expletives and resumptive pronouns can salvage otherwise ill-formed long-distance subject *wh*-movement.

(70) a. *Ver hot er moyre [$_{CP}$ az [vet ⟨ver⟩ kumen]]?   *Yiddish*
        who has he fear   that will   come
        'Who does he fear will come?'
    b. ?Ver hot er moyre [$_{CP}$ az [**es** vet ⟨ver⟩ kumen]]?
        who has he fear   that EXPL will   come
        (= (18a))
        (Diesing 1988:137)

(71) a. *Hvem tror du [$_{CP}$ at [ofte tager til Paris]]?   *Danish*
        who think you   that often goes to Paris
        'Who do you think often goes to Paris?'
        (Vikner 1995:12)
    b. Hvem tror du, [$_{CP}$ at [**der** har gjort det]]?
        who think you   that there has done it
        'Who do you think has done it?'
        (Engdahl 1986:123)

(72) a. *Vilken elev trodde ingen [$_{CP}$ att [skulle fuska]]?   *Swedish*
        which pupil thought nobody   that would cheat
        'Which pupil didn't anyone think would cheat?'
    b. Vilken elev trodde ingen [$_{CP}$ att [**han** skulle fuska]]?
        which pupil thought nobody   that he would cheat
        (Engdahl 1982:166)

French is considered another language of this kind. It has been pointed out that French shows a *que-qui* alternation in long-distance subject *wh*-movement; the movement is well-formed only when the complementizer is *qui*. Consider (73).

(73) a. *Quelles filles crois-tu [$_{CP}$ que [vont ⟨quelles filles⟩ acheter
        which girls think-you   that will   buy
        ce livre-la]]?
        that book-there
        'Which girls do you think will buy that book there?'

b. Quelles filles crois-tu [_CP_ **qui** [vont ⟨quelles filles⟩ acheter ce livre-la]]?
(Taraldsen 2002:29)

Following Taraldsen (2002), we assume that *qui*, as illustrated in (74), is analyzed as the complementizer *que* with the expletive *il*, which is merged in Spec,TP.

(74) ... [que [*i*] [T ...]]] (*i* is an expletive)
⟶ qui

Thus in French (73b), an XP is merged in, just as in (70b) through (72b).

Lack of *that-t* effects in the above examples is correctly predicted by the proposed labeling analysis. In these examples, it can reasonably be considered that XPs (expletives and resumptive pronouns) are merged with the λ-marked set, which is suggested by the fact that the complementizers and the XPs are adjacent to each other. Then, as in subject raising (see section 3.1), the λ-marked set can be labeled by $T_{\{\phi\}}$ with the help of the XPs, which are merged in Spec,TP.[30]

(75) [*wh*P$_{subj}$ [that-C [$_\gamma$ XP$_{\{\phi\}}$ [$_\lambda$ T$_{\{\phi\}}$ [$_\alpha$ ⟨*wh*P$_{subj}$⟩ [$_{v*P}$ ...]..]
(λ = TP; γ = <ϕ, ϕ>)

The examples from (70) through (73) argue that *that-t* effects are not incurred even with overt complementizers when the λ-marked set can be labeled, which endorses the prediction of the proposed analysis.

4.2.3 Labeling by "Topic"

In Yiddish, long-distance subject *wh*-movement does not incur *that-t* effects when non-subject elements are topicalized. Consider the following examples:

---

[30] Some may wonder how ϕ-feature agreement, hence labeling, is executed in (75) if an XP$_{\{\phi\}}$ is not internally but externally merged with the λ-marked set. I argue that agreement can occur as part of labeling (see Abe 2015b, Sorida 2014 for this proposal); given that labeling of XP-YP is executed through minimal detection of agreeing heads (X and Y) and that both Agree and labeling are based on minimal search, agreement or Agree can be implemented as part of labeling of XP-YP (here, the γ-marked set) through minimal detection of shared features. Thus, whether an XP$_{\{\phi\}}$ is internally or externally merged, agreement can be implemented in (75).

(76) a. Ver hot er nit gevolt [$_{CP}$ az [$_\gamma$ ot di bikher [$_\lambda$ zol ⟨ver⟩
who has he not wanted   that   the books   should
leyenen ⟨ot di bikher⟩)]]]?
read
'Who did he not want to read the books?'
(Diesing 1990:75)
  b. ?Ver hot er moyre [$_{CP}$ az [$_\gamma$ haynt [$_\lambda$ vet kumen]]]? (= (18b))
who has he fear   that   today   will come
'Who does he afraid will come?'
(Diesing 1988:138)

Diesing (1990:47) argues that non-subject topics as well as normal subjects can be moved to Spec,TP, with topicalization applying at TP. Then in (76), the object *ot di bikher* 'the books' and the adverb *haynt* 'today' are merged with the λ-marked set and topicalized. What is interesting about (76) is that the SOs merged do not agree with the embedded T$_{\{\phi\}}$: unlike expletives and resumptive pronouns in examples from (70b) through (73b), which we can consider are merged as substitutes for the subjects and can agree with the embedded T$_{\{\phi\}}$ for valuation, the XPs merged in (76) cannot agree with the embedded T$_{\{\phi\}}$ for ϕ valuation. Given that the set of the form XP-YP can only be labeled by minimal detection of X and Y to the extent that they agree (Chomsky 2013:45), the γ-marked set would not be labeled.

I argue that the γ-marked set can be labeled for the topicalization of non-subject elements. I submit that in Yiddish, a topic feature can be assigned to T lexically and that T agrees with non-subject topics in this feature. Thanks to topic agreement, T and non-subject topics are agreeing heads and the γ-marked set can be labeled as "<Top, Top>" by LA through minimal detection of agreeing topic heads when non-subject topics are merged with the λ-marked set.

(77) a. [*wh*P$_{subj}$ [that-C [$_\gamma$ XP$_{\{Top\}}$ [$_\lambda$ T$_{\{Top,\ \phi\}}$ [$_\alpha$ ⟨*wh*P$_{subj}$⟩ [$_{v*P}$ …⟨XP$_{\{Top\}}$⟩
    …]..]   (λ = TP; γ = <Top, Top>)
  b.

```
        WhP_subj
           |
        that-C
            \
         X_{Topic}  YP  T_{Topic, φ}  α
```

Even if an SO merged with the λ-marked set does not agree with T in ϕ-features, the γ-marked set can be labeled for topic agreement. Yiddish has a strategy of assigning a topic feature to T for non-subject topicalization, and the λ-marked set can be labeled without any problems: T is strengthened as a label with the help of topicalized XPs in Spec,TP, which agree with T in a topic feature. In this case, as predicted by the proposed analysis, long-distance subject *wh*-movement does not show *that-t* effects.[31]

4.2.4 Richness of CP Structure

Finally, consider Icelandic, which, as evidenced by (78), is another language which does not show *that-t* effects.

(78) Hver sagðir þú [$_{CP}$ að [$_{λ}$ hefði ⟨hver⟩ borðað þetta epli]]?
 who said you that had eaten this apple
 'Who did you say had eaten this apple?'
 (Maling and Zaenen 1978:480)

To the extent that our proposal is correct, the λ-marked set in (78) is labeled, satisfying Full Interpretation. I argue that the labeling is possible in Icelandic thanks to richness of its left periphery and hence that *that-t* effects do not show up. Icelandic is a V2 language and as illustrated in (79), V2 is observed in the embedded clause as well as in the matrix (in (79), V2ed elements are typed in bold).

(79) a. ... að **bókina** hafa börnin lesið í gær.
 ... that book-the have children-the read yesterday
 '... that the children read the book yesterday.'
 b. ... að **í gær** hafa börnin lesið bókina.
 ... that yesterday have children-the read book-the
 (Vikner 1995:101)

Following the literature (Vikner 1995 among others), I assume that V2 in Icelandic applies at the CP level: that is, V2ed elements are merged with CP and move to its Spec (see also our discussion in section 2.3). Thus, in (79), *bókina* 'the book' and *í gær* 'yesterday' are in the Spec of the embedded CP.

(80) [að [$_{CP}$ [XP$_{V2ed}$] C [T [$_{vP}$ ...]..]

---

[31] Needless to add, "TP" in (17) (i.e., the λ-marked set) can also be labeled thanks to the strategies of λ labeling discussed in sections 4.2.2 and 4.2.3.

This argument is endorsed by (81), which shows that the expletive *það* 'there' can be merged in the embedded clause just as in the matrix clause.

(81) a. ... að   það   hefur   einhver   borðað   epli.
         ... that there has   someone   eaten   apple
         '... that someone has eaten an apple.'
         (Vikner 1995:189)
    b. Það   drekka   margir   vín   á   Íslandi.
       there drink   many [people] wine in Iceland
       'Many people drink wine in Iceland.'
       (Maling and Zaenen 1978:483)

In Icelandic, unlike in English, the expletive can only be merged with CP and is placed in its Spec. As demonstrated in (82), the expletive is ruled out in both embedded and matrix clauses when some element is moved to Spec,CP and V2ed.

(82) a. Hún sagði að   hér   drykkju (*það)   margir   vín.
         she said   that here drink   (there) many [people] wine
         'She said that here many people drink wine.'
    b. Í gær   var (*það) mikill snjór á   jörðinni.
       Yesterday was (there) much   snow on ground-the
       'Yesterday there was much snow on the ground.'
       (Maling and Zaenen 1978:484)

From the discussion above, it can be concluded that V2ed elements are moved to Spec,CP.

With this background in mind, we can reasonably assume that Icelandic allows rich CP structure in the embedded clause, since V2 is possible when the overt complementizer *að* 'that' is present: that is, CP can be layered in the embedded clause, with the overt complementizer being in higher C. I argue that in long-distance subject *wh*-movement, multiple CP structures are produced in the derivation, with the result that the λ-marked set can be labeled through ϕ-feature climbing and *that-t* effects are circumvented. In *that-t* contexts, as in embedded V2 contexts, the overt complementizer *að* is in higher C and feature-climbing of ϕ-features can apply to lower C, where an overt complementizer is not present; ϕ-features can move out of T even when the overt complementizer is present.

(83)   [$_{CP}$ að [$_{CP}$ C$_{\{\phi\}}$ [$_\lambda$ T [$_{vP}$ ...]..]   (λ = TP)

Thanks to the feature climbing, the λ-marked set can be labeled as TP in (83). Since labeling of λ can be executed, *that-t* effects, as predicted, can be circumvented in (78).

The same analysis extends to adverb/anti-adjacency effects in long-distance subject *wh*-movement. As illustrated in (84) and (85), *that-t* effects will disappear even in English when sentential adverbs are merged in the embedded clause. Consider the following examples:

(84) a. Who did she say [that tomorrow [⟨who⟩ would regret his words]]?
b. Which doctor did you tell me [that during an operation [⟨which doctor⟩ had had a heart attack]]?
(Bresnan 1977:194)

(85) a. Robin met the man who Leslie said [that *(for all intents and purposes) [⟨who⟩ was the mayor of the city]].
b. This is the tree which I said [that *(just yesterday) [⟨which⟩ had resisted my shovel]]. (Culicover 1993:98)

Building on Browning (1996) and Watanabe (1993) among others, I assume that sentential adverbs, since they are merged quite high in the clausal structure, motivate CP recursion in the embedded clause: another C head is merged as one element of the clausal architecture and such adverbs are merged with the set headed by that C head and licensed in its Spec (Cinque 1999, Rizzi 1997, 2004). The assumption here is endorsed by the fact that lower C can be overt, with *that* occurring both before and after sentential adverbs. Consider the following example cited from McCloskey (1992):

(86) She maintained *that* when they arrived *that* they would be welcomed.

Since sentential adverbs are merged lower than the complementizer, it can reasonably be assumed that the overt complementizer *that* is in higher C, with lower C being empty, which allows climbing of ϕ-features from T to lower C.

(87) [$_{CP}$ that [$_{CP}$ [S-Adverbial] C$_{\{\phi\}}$ [$_\lambda$ T [$_{vP}$ ...]..] (λ = TP)

As in Icelandic, feature climbing (head movement) can be executed and the λ-marked set can be labeled. In this case, as shown in (84) and (85), *that-t* effects are not observed. It can be concluded that (84) and (85) are well-formed unlike (53a) due to the fact that labeling of the λ-marked set is successful in the former but not in the latter. This endorses the prediction of the proposed analysis of *that-t* effects.

4.2.5 Summary

Wrapping up the discussion in section 4.2, we have seen that long-distance subject *wh*-movement does not always show *that-t* effects. As we have discussed, in cases where *that-t* effects are not observed, the λ-marked set can indeed be labeled. The evidence we have considered here thus confirms the prediction of the proposed analysis, endorsing the argument that *that-t*/ECP effects are reducible to violations of Full Interpretation for a labeling failure.[32]

5 Conclusion

In this paper, I have considered the syntax of subject A′-movement in initial and recursive symbol *S*, and proposed the Vacuous Movement Hypothesis for a subject *wh*-phrase (or an operator subject) under simplest Merge, which is deduced from SMT: the subject is merged with CP, a root of derivation, and does not move to Spec,TP. I have shown that this proposal is theoretically reasonable and is empirically endorsed. I have also proposed that head movement is an upward counterpart to feature inheritance: it is "feature climbing" from lower heads to higher heads. Head movement qua feature climbing derives not only A-properties of a subject *wh*-phrase internally merged in Spec,CP without moving to Spec,TP; it can also solve the problem of labeling of the λ-marked set (informally, "TP") by rendering $T_{\{\phi\}}$ labelable. Finally, I have argued that the ECP effects on the subject (that is, *that-t* effects observed in long-distance subject *wh*-movement) are deducible from the Vacuous Movement Hypothesis and head movement qua feature climbing.

We conclude that simplest Merge (minimal computation in syntax) and labeling by the Labeling Algorithm (Full Interpretation at the interfaces) can deduce both EPP and ECP effects on a subject *wh*-phrase: the EPP and ECP

---

[32] ECP effects on the subject are observed in (ia) as well.

(i) a. *John$_i$ is illegal [t$_i$ to participate].
cf. b. John$_i$ is likely [t$_i$ to participate].

Given Mizuguchi's (2014b) proposal, the ill-formedness of (ia) can also be reduced to violations of Full Interpretation and hence can be deduced from the SMT assumptions. See Mizuguchi (2014b) for details.

phenomena are given principled explanation by a simply designed linguistic system and its interactions with the interface systems. This endorses the assumptions articulated by SMT, and hence upholds the Minimalist hypothesis.

References

Abe, Jun. 2015a. The EPP and subject extraction. *Lingua* 159:1-17.
Abe, Jun. 2015b. Dynamic antisymmetry for labeling. Ms., Tohoku Gakuin University.
Alexiadou, Artemis and Elena Anagnostopoulou. 1998. Parameterizing agr: Word order, V-movement and EPP checking. *Natural Language and Linguistic Theory* 16:491-539.
Bošković, Željko. 2014. Deducing the subject condition, the adjunct condition, the *that*-trace effect and tucking in from labelling. Paper presented at International Workshop in Linguistics, Dokkyo University, 7 November.
Brandi, Luciana and Patrizia Cordin. 1989. Two Italian dialects and the null subject parameter. In *The null subject parameter*, ed. by Osvaldo Jaeggli and Ken Safir, 111-162. Dordrecht: Kluwer.
Bresnan, Joan. 1977. Variables in the theory of transformations. In *Formal syntax*, ed. by Peter Culicover, Thomas Wasow, and Adrian Akmajian, 157-196. New York: Academic Press.
Browning, Marguerite. 1996. CP recursion and *that-t* effects. *Linguistic Inquiry* 27:237-255.
Chomsky, Noam. 1986. *Barriers*. Cambridge, MA: MIT Press.
Chomsky, Noam. 2000. Minimalist inquiries: The framework. In *Step by step: Essays on minimalist syntax in honor of Howard Lasnik*, ed. by Roger Martin, David Michaels, and Juan Uriagereka, 89-155. Cambridge, MA: MIT Press.
Chomsky, Noam. 2004. Beyond explanatory adequacy. In *The cartography of syntactic structures*. Vol. 3, *Structures and beyond*, ed. by Adriana Belletti, 104-131. Oxford: Oxford University Press.
Chomsky, Noam. 2007. Approaching UG from below. In *Interfaces + recursion = language? Chomsky's minimalism and the view from syntax-semantics*, ed. by Uli Sauerland and Hans-Martin Gärtner, 1-29. Berlin: Mouton de Gruyter.
Chomsky, Noam. 2008. On phases. In *Foundational issues in linguistic theory: Essays in honor of Jean-Roger Vergnaud*, ed. by Robert Freidin, Carlos P. Otero, and Maria Luisa Zubizarreta, 133-166. Cambridge, MA: MIT Press.
Chomsky, Noam. 2013. Problems of projection. *Lingua* 130:33-49.
Chomsky, Noam. 2014a. Lecture delivered at Keio Linguistic Colloquium Syntax Session, Keio University, 8 March.
Chomsky, Noam. 2014b. Lecture delivered at MIT, MIT, 19 May.
Chomsky, Noam. 2015. Problems of projection: Extensions. In *Structures, strategies and beyond: Studies in honour of Adriana Belletti*, ed. by Elisa Di Domenico, Cornelia Hamann, and Simona Matteini, 1-16. Amsterdam: John Benjamins.
Cinque, Guglielmo. 1999. *Adverbs and functional heads: A cross-linguistic perspec-

tive. Oxford: Oxford University Press.

van Craenenbroeck, Jeroen and Liliane Haegeman. 2007. The derivation of subject-initial V2. *Linguistic Inquiry* 38:167–178.

Culicover, Peter. 1993. The adverb effect: Evidence against ECP accounts of the *that-t* effect. In *Proceedings of the North East Linguistic Society (NELS) 23*, ed. by Amy J. Schafer, 97–111. Amherst: University of Massachusetts, Graduate Linguistic Student Association.

Diesing, Molly. 1988. Word order and the subject position in Yiddish. In *Proceedings of the North East Linguistic Society (NELS) 18*, ed. by James Blevins and Juli Carter, 124–140. Amherst: University of Massachusetts, Graduate Linguistic Student Association.

Diesing, Molly. 1990. Verb movement and the subject position in Yiddish. *Natural Language and Linguistic Theory* 8:41–79.

Diesing, Molly. 1992. *Indefinites*. Cambridge, MA: MIT Press.

Diesing, Molly. 2004. The upper functional domain in Yiddish. In *Focus on Germanic typology*, ed. by Werner Abraham, 195–209. Berlin: Akademie Verlag.

Engdahl, Elisabet. 1982. Restrictions on unbounded dependencies in Swedish. In *Readings on unbounded dependencies in Scandinavian languages*, ed. by Elisabet Engdahl and Eva Ejerhed, 151–174. Stockholm: Almquist and Wiksell International.

Engdahl, Elisabet. 1986. *Constituent questions: The syntax and semantics of questions with special reference to Swedish*. Dordrecht: Reidel.

Epstein, Samuel D., Hisatsugu Kitahara, and T. Daniel Seely. 2010. Uninterpretable features: What are they and what do they do? In *Exploring crash-proof grammars*, ed. by Michael T. Putnam, 125–142. Amsterdam: John Benjamins.

Epstein, Samuel D., Hisatsugu Kitahara, and T. Daniel Seely. 2012. Structure building that can't be. In *Ways of structure building*, ed. by Myriam Uribe-Etxebarria and Vidal Valmala, 253–270. Oxford: Oxford University Press.

Epstein, Samuel D., Hisatsugu Kitahara, and T. Daniel Seely. 2014. Labeling by minimal search: Implications for successive-cyclic A-movement and the conception of the postulate "phase." *Linguistic Inquiry* 45:463–481.

Erlewine, Michael Yoshitaka. 2014. Anti-locality and Kaqchikel Agent Focus. In *Proceedings of the West Coast Conference on Formal Linguistics (WCCFL) 31*, ed. by Robert E. Santana-LaBarge, 150–159. Somerville, MA: Cascadilla Proceedings Project.

Erlewine, Michael Yoshitaka. 2016. Anti-locality and optimality in Kaqchikel Agent Focus. *Natural Language and Linguistic Theory* 34:429–479.

Fortuny, Jordi. 2008. *The emergence of order in syntax*. Amsterdam: John Benjamins.

van Gelderen, Elly. 2011. *The linguistic cycle: Language change and the language faculty*. Oxford: Oxford University Press.

Givón, Talmy. 1976. Topic, pronoun and grammatical agreement. In *Subject and topic*, ed. by Charles Li, 149–188. New York: Academic Press.

Goto, Nobu. 2013. Labeling and scrambling in Japanese. *Tohoku: Essays and Studies in English Language and Literature* 46:39–73.

Henry, Alison. 1995. *Belfast English and Standard English: Dialect variation and parameter setting*. Oxford: Oxford University Press.
Huybregts, Riny. 2005. Recursively linked case-agreement: From accidents to principles and beyond. In *Organizing grammar: Studies in honor of Henk van Riemsdijk*, ed. by Hans Broekhuis, Norvert Corver, Riny Huybregts, Ursula Kleinhenz, and Jan Koster, 263–274. Berlin: Mouton de Gruyter.
Ishii, Toru. 2004. The phase impenetrability condition, the vacuous, movement hypothesis, and *that-t* effects. *Lingua* 114:183–215.
Jonas, Dianne. 1996. Clause structure and verb syntax in Scandinavian and English. Doctoral dissertation, Harvard University, Cambridge, MA.
Kinyalolo, Kasangati K. W. 1991. *Syntactic dependencies and the spec-head agreement hypothesis in KiLega*. Doctoral dissertation, UCLA, Los Angeles, CA.
Koeneman, Olaf and Ad Neeleman. 2001. Predication, verb movement and the distribution of expletives. *Lingua* 111:189–233.
Koopman, Hilda. 2006. Agreement configurations: In defense of "Spec head." In *Agreement systems*, ed. by Cedric Boeckx, 159–199. Amsterdam: John Benjamins.
Kuroda, Shige-Yuki. 1992. *Japanese syntax and semantics*. Dordrecht: Kluwer.
Lasnik, Howard and Mamoru Saito. 1992. *Move α: Conditions on its application and output*. Cambridge, MA: MIT Press.
Legate, Julie. 2011. Under-inheritance. Paper presented at the 42nd North East Linguistic Society, University of Toronto, 12 November.
Legate, Julie. 2014. *Voice and v: Lessons from Acehnese*. Cambridge, MA: MIT Press.
Maling, Joan and Annie Zaenen. 1978. The nonuniversality of a surface filter. *Linguistic Inquiry* 9:475–497.
Mathew, Rosmin. 2015. *Head movement in syntax*. Amsterdam: John Benjamins.
May, Robert. 1985. *Logical form: Its structure and derivation*. Cambridge, MA: MIT Press.
McCloskey, James. 1992. Adjunction, selection and embedded verb second. Ms., University of California, Santa Cruz.
McCloskey, James. 2000. Quantifier float and *wh*-movement in an Irish English. *Linguistic Inquiry* 31:57–84.
Miyoshi, Nobuhiro. 2009. The EPP, feature inheritance and anti-agreement. In *JELS: Papers from the twenty-sixth conference of the English Linguistic Society of Japan*, ed. by Toshiyuki Tabata et al., 151–160. The English Linguistic Society of Japan.
Mizuguchi, Manabu. 2008. Derivation, minimalism, and *that-trace* effects. *English Linguistics* 25:56–92.
Mizuguchi, Manabu. 2013. Reconsidering phase-internal derivations: Are they exceptional or not? *English Linguistics* 30:75–110.
Mizuguchi, Manabu. 2014a. Phases and counter-cyclicity of A-movement. In *Proceedings of the 16th Seoul international conference on generative grammar (SICOGG)*, ed. by Jong Un Park and Il-Jae Lee, 257–277. The Korean

Generative Grammar Circle.
Mizuguchi, Manabu. 2014b. Superiority effects in minimalism: A case study of A-movement. *English Linguistics* 31:563–582.
Narita, Hiroki. 2014. *Endocentric structuring of projection-free syntax*. Amsterdam: John Benjamins.
Narita, Hiroki and Naoki Fukui. 2014. Symmetry-driven syntax. Ms., Nihon University and Sophia University.
Ogawa, Yoshiki. 2007. C-to-V incorporation and subject raising across CP-boundary. *English Linguistics* 24:33–66.
Ott, Dennis. 2012. *Local instability: Split topicalization and quantifier float in German*. Berlin: Walter de Gruyter.
Ouali, Hamid. 2008. On C-to-T ϕ-feature transfer: The nature of agreement and anti-agreement in Berber. In *Agreement restrictions*, ed. by Roberta D'Alessandro, Susann Fischer, and Gunnar Hrafn Hrafnbjargarson, 159–180. Berlin: Mouton de Gruyter.
Ouhalla, Jamal. 1993. Subject-extraction, negation and the anti-agreement effect. *Natural Language and Linguistic Theory* 11:477–518.
Perlmutter, David. 1971. *Deep and surface structure constraints in syntax*. New York: Holt, Rinehard and Winston.
Rizzi, Luigi. 1982. *Issues in Italian syntax*. Dordrecht: Foris.
Rizzi, Luigi. 1990. *Relativized minimality*. Cambridge, MA: MIT Press.
Rizzi, Luigi. 1997. The fine structure of the left periphery. In *Elements of grammar: Handbook of generative syntax*, ed. by Liliane Haegeman, 281–337. Dordrecht: Kluwer.
Rizzi, Luigi. 2004. Locality and left periphery. In *The cartography of syntactic structures*. Vol. 3, *Structures and beyond*, ed. by Adriana Belletti, 223–251. Oxford: Oxford University Press.
Rizzi, Luigi. 2006. On the form of chains: Criterial positions and ECP effects. In *WH-movement: Moving on*, ed. by Lisa Lai-Shen Cheng and Norbert Corver, 97–133. Cambridge, MA: MIT Press.
Rizzi, Luigi. 2014. Some consequences of criterial freezing: Asymmetries, anti-adjacency, and extraction from cleft sentences. In *The cartography of syntactic structures*. Vol. 9, *Functional structure from top to toe*, ed. by Peter Svenonius, 19–45. Oxford: Oxford University Press.
Rizzi, Luigi and Ur Shlonsky. 2007. Strategies of subject extraction. In *Interfaces + recursion = language? Chomsky's minimalism and the view from syntax-semantics*, ed. by Uli Sauerland and Hans-Martin Gärtner, 115–160. Berlin: Mouton de Gruyter.
Roberts, Ian. 2010a. A deletion analysis of null subjects. In *Parametric variation: Null subjects in minimalist theory*, ed. by Theresa Biberauer, Anders Holmberg, Ian Roberts, and Michelle Sheehan, 58–87. Cambridge: Cambridge University Press.
Roberts, Ian. 2010b. *Agreement and head movement: Clitics, incorporation, and defective goals*. Cambridge, MA: MIT Press.

Roberts, Ian and Anders Holmberg. 2010. Introduction: Parameters in minimalist theory. In *Parametric variation: Null subjects in minimalist theory*, ed. by Theresa Biberauer, Anders Holmberg, Ian Roberts, and Michelle Sheehan, 1–57. Cambridge: Cambridge University Press.

Schneider-Zioga, Patricia. 2007. Anti-agreement, anti-locality and minimality: The syntax of dislocated subjects. *Natural Language and Linguistic Theory* 25:403–446.

Schwartz, Bonnie D. and Sten Vikner. 1989. All verb second clauses are CPs. *Working Papers in Scandinavian Syntax* 43:27–49.

Schwartz, Bonnie D. and Sten Vikner. 1996. The verb always leaves IP in V2 clauses. In *Parameters and functional heads: Essays in comparative syntax*, ed. by Adriana Belletti and Luigi Rizzi, 11–62. Oxford: Oxford University Press.

Simpson, Andrew and Zoe Wu. 2001. Agreement, shells, and focus. *Language* 78:287–313.

Sorida, Masanobu. 2014. Multiple-branching structures in syntax. In *Proceedings of the 16th Seoul international conference on generative grammar (SICOGG)*, ed. by Jong Un Park and Il-Jae Lee, 411–419. The Korean Generative Grammar Circle.

Taraldsen, Knut Tarald. 2002. The *que/qui* alternation and the distribution of expletives. In *Subjects, expletives, and the EPP*, ed. by Peter Svenonius, 29–42. Oxford: Oxford University Press.

Vikner, Sten. 1995. *Verb movement and expletive subjects in the Germanic languages*. Oxford: Oxford University Press.

Watanabe, Akira. 1993. Larsonian CP recursion, factive complements, and selection. In *Proceedings of the North East Linguistic Society (NELS) 23*, ed. by Amy J. Schafer, 523–537. Amherst: University of Massachusetts, Graduate Linguistic Student Association.

Labeling Ambiguity in the Root Context and Sentence-Final Particles*

Miyoko Yasui and Yoshiro Asayama

This paper argues for the positive roles of selection in labeling syntactic objects (SOs) formed of non-heads by free Merge. A standard minimalist account is that movement of one of the non-heads and feature agreement in its landing site yield labeled SOs to be transferred to the PF/LF interfaces cyclically at each phase. If selection also plays crucial roles in labeling, the root/embedded asymmetry is expected since a root by definition is not selected. Sentence-final particles in East Asian languages present an interesting case of labeling ambiguity in the root context; these languages lack overt agreement, and their particles can appear in the middle as well as at the end of a sentence. It is argued that the distributional versatility of the particles is deducible from their unrestricted selectional properties and their existence necessarily follows from the lack of agreement in the C-T domain.

Keywords: multiple outputs, selection, root phenomena, agreement

1 Labeling Algorithms in the Minimalist Framework

Chomsky (2008) has initiated an explicit attempt to eliminate X-bar theoretic stipulations on the labeling of a syntactic object (SO) formed of α and β by the following version of 'minimal search' mechanism:

(1) (i) If α is a lexical item, α is the label of SO.
 (ii) If SO results from the internal merger of α to β, the label of β is the label of SO.

(1i,ii) are assumed to be non-overlapping in the standard X-bar theory. Drawing on Donati (2005), Chomsky discusses that both (1i,ii) are applicable

---

* Earlier versions of this paper were presented at International Linguistics Workshop held at Dokkyo University on November 7, 2014 and at the Annual Meeting of the Society of Japanese Grammar held at Gakushuin Women's College on November 15, 2015. We would like to thank the audiences at the two conferences, especially Hiroshi Aoyagi for elaborating our Korean data. The research reported in this paper was supported by Dokkyo University under International Research Grant.

if a head is internally merged. More specifically, if a *wh*-word merges with an SO headed by a [WH] C as in (2a,b), the result can be labeled by either lexical item according to (1i,ii), and the two labels are semantically compatible with interrogative and non-interrogative predicates, whereas if a complex *wh*-phrase is merged as in (3a,b), only (1ii) can apply, which causes a selectional violation in (3b).

(2) a. I wonder [$_\gamma$ [$_D$ what] [$_{CP}$ [$_C$ WH] you wrote]] (γ = CP)
    b. I read [$_\gamma$ [$_D$ what] [$_{CP}$ [$_C$ WH] you wrote]] (γ = DP)

(3) a. I wonder [$_\gamma$ [$_{DP}$ what book] [$_{CP}$ [$_C$ WH] you wrote]] (γ = CP)
    b. *I read [$_\gamma$ [$_{DP}$ what book] [$_{CP}$ [$_C$ WH] you wrote]] (γ = CP)

(1i), which was assumed in traditional grammars and X-bar theories, is retained in the more recent minimalist framework (Chomsky 2013, 2015 among others). The stipulative residue in (1ii) has been restated in terms of prominent feature sharing (or more simply agreement) between α and β; the *wh*-feature shared by *what/what book* and the [WH] C in (2a) and (3a) becomes the label of γ. Unlike in (2a,b), a complex phrase is moved successive-cyclically in (3a,b), involving merger of two non-heads at each step, to which (1i) is not applicable. It is argued that the moving phrase allows the target phrase to label the SO it forms by further moving out of the SO; a full category can label but not its copy. The iterative merger of *what book* in (3a,b) stops at the embedded CP, where it shares the *wh*-feature with a projection of the [WH] C; the SO labeled by the interrogative *wh*-feature can merge only with interrogative predicates like *wonder* to be interpretable at the C-I interface.

In this way, the core insights in (1i,ii) have been incorporated into the current minimalist framework, but what about the idea that a single pair of SOs can potentially be labeled by either SO? The labeling ambiguity in (2a,b) is claimed to come from the structurally minimal status of the moving element *what*. Citing Moro (2000) and Alexiadou and Anagnostopolou (2001), Chomsky (2013:43–44) argues that merger of two non-heads can result in different derivations from the same set of lexical items, as exemplified in (4).

(4) a. The towers of a town appeared in the distance.
    b. In the distance appeared the towers of a town.

The derivation of (4a,b) involves structure α in (5a,b), which results from merger of two phrases: [_DP_ the towers of a town] and [_PP_ in the distance].[1]

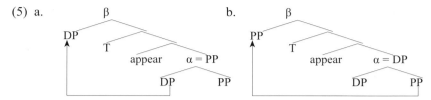

After α merges with the unaccusative verb *appear* and further with T, either DP or PP moves out of α to let the remaining phrase label α. β is again composed of two non-heads, but sharing of φ- or some prominent feature between the DP/PP and a projection of T is argued to dissolve the labeling ambiguity.[2]

Note that the label of γ in (2a,b) should be fixed immediately before γ undergoes further merger; otherwise, the selectional/θ-marking requirements would not be verifiable.[3] On the other hand, α in (5a,b) is unlabeled at the stage where it merges with *appear*; it is labeled only after one of its constituents moves out and merges with a projection of T, forming β. This delay of labeling is allowed if transfer to the two interfaces is restricted to phases, which include CP, *v*P, and probably DP; unaccusative predicates like *appear* lack a strong light verb. What about the selectional/θ-marking requirement of the verb *appear* before and after the label of α is determined? *Appear* in (5a,b) has the meaning 'begin to be seen', which is semantically compatible only with a locative complement like *in the distance*; thus, the selectional/θ-marking restriction of *appear* is satisfied in (5a) but not in (5b) at the stage where the label of α is fixed. The acceptability of (5b) might suggest that merging *appear* with an unlabeled SO cannot cause a selectional violation simply because the SO has no label and that selectional requirements matter only immediately upon initial mergers. Still, the PP fails to be θ-marked by *appear* after the movement or in situ in (5b). This is one of the issues to be explored in this paper.

There are well-known asymmetries between (5a,b). First, Emonds

---

[1] The verbalizing head *v* and other details are omitted in (5a,b).
[2] Chomsky (2015:9) argues that either DP or PP must move to merge with a projection of T since T in English alone is "too weak" to serve as a label.
[3] We assume that Merge applies unrestrictively, but its output should be interpretable at the sensory-motor (SM) and conceptual-intentional (CI) interfaces. Selectional/θ-marking requirements here should be understood in this sense.

(1970:12, 23) observes that the inversion in (5b), referred to as locative inversion, is disallowed in most embedded clauses; the (b) examples below are much worse than the (a) examples with canonical word order:

(6) a. I was surprised when the dog trotted up.
 b. *I was surprised when up trotted the dog.

(7) a. I have no ideas how often John and his family sat among the guests.
 b. *I have no ideas how often among the guests sat John and his family.

(8) a. Now that a large wicker couch is on the porch, we can all relax.
 b. *Now that on the porch is a large wicker couch, we can all relax.

Bresnan (1994:108) elaborates the generalization made by Emonds, claiming that locative inversion is allowed in those finite clauses where topicalization is possible. In other words, it is totally excluded in infinitive and gerundive clauses.

(9) a. I expect a picture of Leonard Pabbs to be hung on this wall.
 b. *I expect on this wall to be hung a picture of Leonard Pabb.

(10) a. I anticipated a picture of Leonard Pabbs being hung on this wall.
 b. *I anticipated on this wall being hung a picture of Leonard Pabbs.

Second, locative inversion does not co-occur with the subject-auxiliary inversion.

(11) a. Is my brother sitting in the room?
 b. *Is in the room sitting my brother?

(12) a. Did the baby roll down the hill?
 b. *Did down the hill roll the baby?
 (Rizzi and Shlonsky 2006:344)

It is not the case that locative inversion is excluded in questions; *wh*-questions are possible if the inverted PP is a *wh*-phrase and the subject-auxiliary inversion does not occur:

(13) a. Out of which barn ran a horse?
 b. *Out of which barn did run a horse?
 (Hoekstra and Mulder 1990:32)

Thus, the restriction observed in (11) and (12) is not semantic but syntactic in nature. The cartographic approach advocated in Rizzi and Shlonsky (2006) and related work attributes the peculiarities of locative inversion to some abstract heads in the left periphery of finite clauses. Bresnan's (1994) insights fall under this line of analyses. Another possibility is to capture the root/embedded distinction in terms of labeling and selection: a root clause by definition is not selected and need not necessarily be labeled in the same manner as embedded constituents.[4] Then, the marginal status of (5b) in the embedded clause is expected to be reducible to some selectional violation between β and a higher head.

A typical root sentence like (14) consists of two non-heads, which should cause labeling ambiguity, as discussed by Chomsky (2013:39). It is necessary to explain why the interrogative counterpart of (14) should involve the movement of V rather than N as shown in (15), given that the two heads are indistinguishable for minimal search from outside α.

(14)   [$_\alpha$ [$_{NP}$ young [$_N$ eagles]] [$_{TP}$ [$_T$ are] flying]]

(15) a. *[eagles [$_\alpha$ [$_{NP}$ young <eagles>] [$_{TP}$ are flying]]]?
     b. [are [$_\alpha$ [$_{NP}$ young eagles] [$_{TP}$ <are> flying]]]?

The contrast in (15a,b) suggests that the label of α is decided uniquely, unlike γ in (2a,b) and α in (5a,b). Note that multiple labeling is not possible if a simple D is merged with TP unlike in (2a,b).

(16) a. *I met [$_\alpha$ [$_D$ it] [$_{TP}$ was raining]]
     b. *I met [$_\alpha$ [$_D$ he] [$_{TP}$ came]]
     c. *I met [$_\alpha$ [$_D$ him] [$_{TP}$ to be honest]]

(16a,b) could be ruled out for θ- and Case-theoretic reasons, respectively, but (16c) would be innocuous if α were labeled DP. What seems to be wrong with (16c) as well as (15a) is that a TP fails to be selected by a C or higher verb.

The foregoing brief review of labeling algorithms proposed in the minimalist framework converges on the question: What factors conspire to deter-

---

[4] Chomsky (2008) claims that the labeling ambiguity needs to be resolved for the SO to enter into the computation. Then, {XP, YP} as a root clause does not require a unique label since by definition it undergoes no further computation. Chomsky (2013:43), on the other hand, attributes the labeling necessity to the interpretive requirements of SOs at the interfaces. As will be discussed in the last section, a root clause corresponds to one of the important elements in the formal definition of a language: the initial symbol. Then, its labeling can be regarded as falling outside the general labeling algorithms.

mine whether an unlabeled SO formed of non-heads by free Merge yields a single output or multiple outputs. It has been standardly acknowledged in current minimalist research that movement of one of the non-heads and feature agreement in its landing site are key mechanisms to resolve labeling ambiguity. The role of selection by higher heads of unlabeled SOs does not seem to have attracted much attention except for ambiguous cases between *wh*-questions and *wh*-relatives exemplified by (2a,b). If selection plays crucial roles in resolving labeling ambiguity, the root/embedded asymmetry is expected since a root by definition is not selected. With these issues in mind, we will take up sentence-final (S-final) particles in Japanese and other East Asian languages, showing that they typically appear at the end of root clauses but may also attach to embedded constituents. In other words, multiple PF outputs are obtained from merger with S-final particles, just as in (2a,b) and (5a,b), and crucially unlike in (15a,b) and (16). More importantly, these languages lack φ-feature agreement in the TP domain and overt *wh*-movement in the CP domain; hence, iterative applications of free Merge presumably do not halt via feature agreement as argued by Saito (2014). We will argue that the selectional properties of S-final particles allow the derivation to stop in more than one way.

The rest of this paper is organized as follows. Section 2 demonstrates that some of the S-final particles in Japanese can appear after (i) S-final predicates, (ii) S-final non-predicative phrases, and (iii) S-internal phrases. Assuming usages (ii) and (iii) to show that the particles do not necessarily select SOs labeled by a finite predicate, we will argue that their selectional properties make S-final and S-internal usages possible in their merger with a SO consisting of two non-heads, which is a typical case of labeling ambiguity. Sections 3 and 4 render support for this line of analysis by showing that S-final particles in Old Japanese as well as many other East Asian languages behave like those in modern Japanese. Section 5 elaborates the proposal given in Section 2 with special attention to the historical change of the S-final particle *ka*. Section 6 concludes by offering a preliminary answer to the empirically and theoretically important question: Why do Japanese and other East Asian languages have S-final particles that allow multiple outputs in the root context, while most European languages do not?

2 S-internal Usage of S-final Particles in Japanese

As their name suggests, S-final particles (SFPs) in Japanese such as *ne*, *yo*, *sa*, and *na* occur at the end of sentences as in (17a,b) and are excluded in embedded clauses except for direct quotations as in (17c,d).

(17) a. Taro-ga   Hanako-kara sakuzitu   kono tegami-o   morat-ta
       Taro-NOM Hanako-from yesterday this   letter-ACC receive-PAST
       ne/yo/sa/na.
       SFP
       'Taro received this letter from Hanako yesterday.'
   b. Taro-wa   seiseki-ga   yokat-ta   ne/yo/sa/na.
      Taro-TOP grade-NOM   good-PAST   SFP
      'Taro made good grades.'
   c. *Watasi-wa [Taro-ga   seiseki-ga   yokat-ta]   ne/yo/sa/na
      I-TOP   Taro-NOM   grades-NOM good-PAST   SFP
      no-o   sitteiru.
      NO-ACC   know
      'I know that Taro made good grades.'
   d. *[Taro-ga   ie-o   de-ta]   ne/yo/sa/na toki, Hanako-wa
       Taro-NOM   home-ACC leave-PAST SFP   when   Hanako-TOP
      netei-ta.
      sleeping-PAST
      'When Taro left home, Hanako was asleep.'

The S-final particles in (17a,b) attach to finite predicates. They can also follow nouns, postpositions and adverbs, which do not inflect for tense.

(18) a. Hanako-kara sakuzitu   kono tegami-o   morat-ta   no-wa
       Hanako-from yesterday this   letter-ACC receive-PAST NO-TOP
       Taro   ne/yo/sa/na.
       Taro   SFP
       'It is Taro who received this letter from Hanako yesterday.'
   b. Taro-ga   sakuzitu   kono tegami-o   morat-ta   no-wa
      Taro-NOM yesterday this   letter-ACC receive-PAST NO-TOP
      Hanako-kara   ne/yo/sa/na.
      Hanako-from SFP
      'It is from Hanako that Taro received this letter yesterday.'
   c. Taro-ga   Hanako-kara kono tegami-o   morat-ta   no-wa
      Taro-NOM Hanako-from this   letter-ACC receive-PAST NO-TOP
      sakuzitu   ne/yo/sa/na.
      yesterday SFP
      'It is yesterday that Taro received this letter from Hanako.'

(18a–c) are cleft sentences based on (17a). The focused phrases in (18a–c) can be put back to where they canonically appear with a pause after the S-final particle.

(19) a. Taro-ga   ne/yo/sa/na, Hanako-kara sakuzitu kono tegami-o
       Taro-NOM SFP   Hanako-from yesterday this letter-ACC
       morat-ta.[5]
       receive-PAST
   b. Taro-ga Hanako-kara ne/yo/sa/na, sakuzitu kono tegami-o morat-ta.
   c. Taro-ga Hanako-kara sakuzitu ne/yo/sa/na, kono tegami-o morat-ta.

For ease of illustration, the three usages of S-final particles attached to S-final predicates in (17a,b), to S-final non-predicative phrases in (18a–c), and to S-internal phrases in (19a–c) are to be referred to as usages (i)–(iii), respectively. Except for the interrogative marker *ka*, S-final particles in general do not have much lexical content but express some attitudes of the speaker on the utterance such as confirmation, approval, and consent. The functions of the S-final particles appear to be essentially the same among the three usages, though the phrases they attach to are focused in (19a–c) just as in the clefts (18a–c), while (17a,b) are neutral in this respect.

Focusing on (17a) and (19a) for the moment, they can be regarded as instantiating interesting cases of labeling ambiguity. Suppose that the matrix clause α consists of two phrases (XP and YP) and α merges with a S-final particle, as represented in (20a), where P stands for the particle.

(20)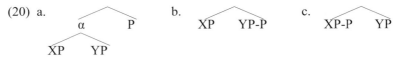

If P can select either constituent of α and the selection is morphologically realized as suffixation of P to the constituent it selects, two outputs (20b,c) are obtained from (20a), which correspond to S-final and S-internal usages, respectively; usages (i) and (ii) fall under (20b), and usage (iii) under (20c). The innocuous labeling ambiguity here sharply contrasts with the non-ambiguity of English matrix TPs discussed in connection to (15a,b). In (15a), which is totally outrageous, the interrogative C erroneously attracts the head

---

[5] Admitting that the S-internal usage of *yo* sounds highly vulgar whereas the S-final *yo* is not, the two instances of *yo* are to be treated as the same particle here.

of the subject, while the S-final particle can be associated with the subject in (19a), which is colloquial but perfectly acceptable. We will eventually deduce this difference from the obligatoriness of finite tenses in English matrix clauses.

Before going into this central issue, it is necessary to see to what extent usages (ii) and (iii) are parallel. First of all, Masuoka and Takubo (1992) point out that both usages allow the copula *da* and its polite form *desu* to appear before the particles.

(21) a. Hanako-kara sakuzitu kono tegami-o morat-ta   no-wa
    Hanako-from yesterday this   letter-ACC receive-PAST NO-TOP
    Taro da   ne/yo/na.[6]
    Taro COP SFP
    'It is Taro who received this letter from Hanako yesterday.'
 b. Taro-ga da ne/yo/na, Hanako-kara sakujitsu kono tegami-o morat-ta.

(22) a. Taro-ga   sakuzitu kono tegami-o morat-ta   no-wa
    Taro-NOM yesterday this   letter-ACC receive-PAST NO-TOP
    Hanako-kara desu   ne/yo/na.
    Hanako-from COP.POLITE SFP
    'It is from Hanako that Taro received this letter yesterday.'
 b. Taro-ga Hanako-kara desu ne/yo/na, sakuzitu kono tegami-o morat-ta.

(23) a. Taro-ga Hanako-kara kono tegami-o morat-ta   no-wa
    Taro-NOM Hanako-from this   letter-ACC receive-PAST NO-TOP
    sakuzitu da   ne/yo/na.
    yesterday COP SFP
    'It is yesterday that Taro received this letter from Hanako.'
 b. Taro-ga Hanako-kara sakuzitu da ne/yo/na, kono tegami-o morat-ta.

S-final usage (ii), however, differs from S-internal usage (iii) in that case particles are optional or tend to be avoided before the particles in the former but need to be retained in the latter.

---

[6] *Sa* is impossible if preceded by copulas. *Sa* in the subsequent examples is to be understood to obey this restriction.

(24) a. Hanako-kara sakuzitu   kono tegami-o morat-ta   no-wa
        Hanako-from yesterday   this letter-ACC receive-PAST NO-TOP
        Taro-*ga/∅ (da) ne.
        Taro-NOM   COP SFP
        'It is Taro who received this letter from Hanako yesterday.'
    b. Taro-ga/*∅ (da) ne/yo/sa/na, Hanako-kara sakuzitu kono tegami-o morat-ta.

(25) a. Taro-ga   Hanako-kara sakuzitu   morat-ta   no-wa   kono
        Taro-NOM   Hanako-from yesterday   receive-PAST   NO-TOP   this
        tegami-*o/∅ (desu)   ne.
        letter-ACC COP.POLITE SFP
        'It is this letter that Taro received from Hanako yesterday.'
    b. Taro-ga Hanako-kara sakuzitu kono tegami-o/*∅ (desu) ne, morat-ta.

(26) a. Taro-ga   sakuzitu   kono tegami-o watasi-ta no-wa   Hanako
        Taro-NOM   yesterday   this letter-ACC hand-PAST NO-TOP Hanako
        ni/∅ (da) ne.
        to   COP SFP
        'It is to Hanako that Taro handed this letter yesterday.'
    b. Taro-ga Hanako-ni/*∅ (da) ne, sakuzitu kono tegami-o watasi-ta.

(27) a. Taro-ga   kono nimotu-o   okut-ta   no-wa   Hanako-no
        Taro-NOM   this luggage-ACC send-PAST   NO-TOP Hanako-GEN
        zikka   e/∅ (da) ne.
        parents' home to   COP SFP
        'It is to Hanako's parents' home that Taro sent this luggage.'
    b. Taro-ga kono nimotu-o Hanako-no zikka e/*∅ (da) ne, okut-ta.

Another difference is that the past forms of the copulas are perfect in S-final usage (ii) but are highly unnatural in S-internal usage (iii).

(28) a. Taro-ga   sakuzitu   kono tegami-o morat-ta   no-wa
        Taro-NOM   yesterday   this letter-ACC receive-PAST   NO-TOP
        Hanako   kara   dat-ta   ne.
        Hanako   from   COP-PAST   SFP
        'It was from Hanako that Taro received this letter yesterday.'
    b. *Taro-ga Hanako-kara dat-ta ne, sakuzitu kono tegami-o morat-ta.

One could argue that the particles under S-internal usage (iii) constitute an independent category simply because they do not appear S-finally.[7] As has been shown in (18) and (19), however, the particles in S-final usage (ii) can attach to the same range of categories as those in S-internal usage (iii); they do not c-select a specific category or have a θ-marking property. In the next two sections, we will demonstrate that Old Japanese and other East Asian languages have S-final particles that allow usages (i)–(iii). Therefore, instead of setting up two distinct categories, we will assume usages (i)–(iii) to undergo essentially the same derivation and work out in the current minimalist framework why Japanese S-final particles exhibit such versatile properties. The important observations made in this section are: Japanese S-final particles such as *ne* impose no selectional/θ-marking requirement on a SO they merge with, attaching not only to finite predicates but also to non-predicative phrases that can bear no inflection, and the past forms of copulas are allowed after S-final non-predicates in usage (ii) but disallowed in S-internal usage (iii). S-final particles are often treated on a par with complementizers like *whether* and *if* in English, but they are quite different in that they have little or no necessity to be associated with tense morphemes.

3 S-final Particles in Old Japanese

Old Japanese (OJ) had several particles that appeared S-finally and expressed a certain kind of the speaker's attitude. Some of them required the predicate to take a specific conjugational form. This phenomenon is known as Kakarimusubi. In this section, we will take up four of the Kakari particles *ka*, *zo*, *ya*, and *wa*, as well as one non-Kakari particle *yo* mainly in Chuko (Nara and Heian) Period, and show that they had the three usages observed with the S-final particles in modern Japanese (MJ): (i) after S-final predicates, (ii) after S-final non-predicative phrases, and (iii) after S-internal phrases.[8]

Let us first look at the three usages of the interrogative marker *ka*. They are given in (29)–(31), where the conjugational distinctions on predicates are

---

[7] The category in question is called interjective particle.

[8] All the examples in Old Japanese come from *Nihon Koten-bungaku Taikei Honbun Deeta Beesu* (Text Database of Old Japanese Literature) managed by Kokubungaku Kenkyuu Shiryookan available at http://base3.nijl.ac.jp/, except for (29a) and (44), which are taken from *Japanese Text Initiative* at Virginia University available at http://jti.lib.virginia.edu/japanese/index.euc.html, and (35a) from *Aozorabunko* available at http://www.aozora.gr.jp/.

not explicitly glossed here but will be discussed in Section 5.3.

(29) *Ka* in usage (i)
    a. Uta   yomase   tamai   turu   <u>ka</u>.
       poem compose HONORIF PERF Q
       'Have you composed poems?'
       (*Makura-no Sosi*:84)
    b. Kyakuzin-wa ne   tamai   nuru   <u>ka</u>.
       guest-TOP   sleep HONORIF PERF Q
       'Has the guest slept?'
       (*Genji Monogatari*:Hahakigi)

(30) *Ka* in usage (ii)
    a. Inoti tuki namu to suru-wa mae-no   yo-no   mukui
       life   end PERF C do-TOP previous-GEN life-GEN retribution
       <u>ka</u>.
       Q
       'Is it due to the retribution of my previous life that my present life seems to be going to end?'
       (*Genji Monogatari*:Akashi)
    b. Konogoro hito-no   iu   koto-wa makoto <u>ka</u>.
       recently people-NOM talk thing-TOP truth   Q
       'Is what people say recently true?'
       (*Izumi Sikibu Nikki*)

(31) *Ka* in usage (iii)
    a. Nan-no   eki   <u>ka</u>-wa haberamu.
       what-GEN benefit Q-TOP exist
       'What benefits are there?'
       (*Genji Monogatari*:Usugumo)
    b. Sono hito   to   ware to idure-o   <u>ka</u> omou.
       that person or I   or which-ACC Q   love
       'That person or me, which do you love?'
       (*Yamato Monogatari*:141)

It should be noted that like the OJ counterparts, S-final instances of *ka* in MJ are interrogative as shown in (32a,b), whereas S-internal *ka* constitutes an indefinite phrase as shown in (32c).

(32) a. Dare-ga kotira ni kuru <u>ka</u>.
       who-NOM here to come Q

'Who comes here?'
b. Kotira ni kuru-no-wa dare ka.
here to come-NO-TOP who Q
'Who is the one coming here?'
c. Dare-ka kotira ni kuru.
who-INDEF here to come.
'Someone is coming here.'

Ka in OJ did not change its essential meaning according to its syntactic positions just like the four S-final particles in MJ discussed in the previous section.

Zo, expressing the speaker's certainty, also had the three usages as illustrated in (33)–(35).

(33) *Zo* in usage (i)
    a. Ko-wa nadeu koto-o notamau zo.
       this-TOP what.sort.of thing-ACC say.HONORIF SFP
       'What kind of thing do you say?'
       (*Taketori Monogatari*)
    b. Tada hito-ni katar-e tote kikasuru zo.
       just person-DAT talk-IMPERATIVE C tell SFP
       'I will tell this to you, just expecting you to tell it to someone.'
       (*Makura-no Sosi*:82)

(34) *Zo* in usage (ii)
    a. Idesase tamau-wa iduti zo.
       go.out HONORIF-TOP where SFP
       'Where in the world would you go?'
       (*Izumi Shikibu Nikki*)
    b. Tuki-o yumihari-to iu-wa nani-no kokoro zo.
       moon-ACC bow-C call-TOP what-GEN meaning SFP
       'What is really the reason why you call the moon "bow"?'
       (*Yamato Monogatari*:132)

(35) *Zo* in usage (iii)
    a. Koyoi-no tuki-wa umi ni zo iru.
       tonight-GEN moon-TOP sea to SFP set
       'I'm sure tonight's moon will set in the sea.'
       (*Tosa Nikki*)
    b. Tuyu-no wa-ga mi zo ayauku, ...
       dewdrop-GEN I-GEN body SFP fragile

'My life, which is like a dewdrop, is really fragile, ...'
(*Izumi Shikibu Nikki*)

Zo in MJ appears S-finally and expresses the speaker's certainty as in (36a), but it lacks the other two usages as shown in (36b,c).

(36) a. Taro-ga   Hanako-ni   kossori   hon-o   age-ta   zo.
    Taro-NOM Hanako-DAT secretly book-ACC give-PAST SFP
    'Taro gave a book to Hanako secretly.'
 b. *Hanako-ni kossori hon-o ageta-no-wa Taro zo.
    'It is Taro who gave a book to Hanako secretly.'
 c. *Taro-ga zo, Hanako-ni kossori hon-o age-ta.

(36b), if acceptable at all, sounds extremely archaic.[9] (36c) shows that *zo* cannot attach to S-internal phrases.

OJ had two kinds of interrogative markers *ka* and *ya*. In usage (iii), *ka* attached basically to *wh*-phrases, whereas *ya* attached to non-*wh*-phrases, making alternate questions on the already known fact. *Ya* appears to have allowed the three usages in Heian Period as shown in (37)–(38).

(37) *Ya* in usage (i)
 a. Sakuya-wa   mairi   ki-tari-to-wa   kiki
    last.night-TOP 1STPERSON come-PERF-C-TOP hear
    tamai   kemu   ya.
    2NDPERSON.HONORIF seem.to.have SFP
    'You seem to have heard that I came last night, don't you?'
    (*Izumi Shikibu Nikki*)
 b. Kakisigure-taru   momizi-no   taguinaku zo   miyu ya.
    rain.suddenly-PERF autumn.leave-NOM rare   SFP look SFP
    'Autumn leaves, which have had sudden rain, look very wonderful, do they?'
    (*Sarashina Nikki*)

---

[9] (36b) becomes acceptable if *zo* is preceded by a copula.
  (i) Hanako-ni   kossori   hon-o   age-ta-no-wa   Taro da   zo.
      Hanako-DAT secretly book-ACC give-Past-NO-TOP Taro COP SFP
      'It is Taro who gave a book to Hanako secretly.'

Na, ze, and *wa* in MJ behave similarly.

(38) *Ya* in usage (ii)
    a. Ayasi-no   ayumi   ya.
        mystery-GEN walking   SFP
        'It is a strange walking, isn't it?'
        (*Izumi Shikibu Nikki*)
    b. Kisaki-no   tadani   owasi-keru   toki to   ya.
        queen-NOM commoner be.HONORIF-PAST time C   SFP
        '(I heard that) it was when the queen had been a commoner, wasn't it.'
        (*Ise Monogatari*:6)

(39) *Ya* in usage (iii)
    a. Kokoro-o   ya   kiki-etari   kemu.
        mind-ACC   SFP   comprehend-able seem.to.have
        'He seems to have been able to comprehend my feelings, doesn't he?'
        (*Tosa Nikki*)
    b. Housi ni   ya   narini   kemu
        priest to   SFP   become seem.to.have
        'He seems to have become a priest, doesn't he?'
        (*Yamato Monogatari*:168)

Oono (1993:261, 269) points out that *ya* in *Manyo-shu* written in Nara Period did not attach to S-final non-predicative phrases, lacking usage (ii), but a few examples like (38a,b) were attested later in Heian Period. We assume that *ya* had the function of making an alternate question in all the three usages in OJ.

   Yo in OJ had no transparent meaning or discourse function like its MJ counterpart. It had the three usages in OJ just as in MJ:

(40) *Yo* in usage (i)
    a. Koyoi-wa   makari namu   yo.
        tonight-TOP   go   will   SFP
        'I will certainly go tonight.'
        (*Ise Monogatari*)
    b. Saru kokoti-ni   dousin okosite tukiaruku-ramu   yo.
        that thought-by faith   get   walk.around-will   SFP
        'He seems to have become religious because of that thought, and is walking around.'
        (*Makura-no Sosi*:43)

(41) *Yo* in usage (ii)
    a. Saru uta-no kitanagesa <u>yo</u>.
        that poem-GEN dishonorableness SFP
        'How dishonorable that poem is!'
        (*Ise Monogatari*:103)
    b. Hitotu-wa kono sugi tamainisi onkoto <u>yo</u>.
        first-TOP this pass HONORIF.PAST affair SFP
        'The first one is this past affair.'
        (*Genji Monogatari*:Usugumo)

(42) *Yo* in usage (iii)
    a. Kore-ga na <u>yo</u> ikani.
        this-GEN name SFP what
        'What is this name?'
        (*Makura-no Sosi*:93)
    b. Kuyuru kemuri <u>yo</u> yukukata zo naki.
        wafting smoke SFP destination SFP not.exist
        'Wafting smoke has no destination.'
        (*Genji Monogatari*:Suma)

Finally, we speculate that the Kakari particle *wa* is the same morpheme as the S-final particle *wa* though they are usually treated as separate lexical items. If they are in fact the same, *wa* can be regarded as showing the three usages at stake as follows.

(43) *Wa* in usage (i)
    a. Kono koto hitobito mousu naru <u>wa</u>.
        this matter people talk ASSERTIVE SFP
        'This matter, people are talking about.'
        (*Izumi Shikibu Nikki*)
    b. On'okuri tukoumaturi-turu <u>wa</u>.
        send.HONORIF modest-PERF SFP
        'I humbly send this to you.'
        (*Genji Monogatari*:Suetsumuhana)

(44) *Wa* in usage (ii)
    Hito-no togamu beki koto ka <u>wa</u>.
    people-NOM blame should matter Q SFP
    'Isn't it what people should blame?'
    (*Makura-no Sosi*:28)

(45) *Wa* in usage (iii)
    a. Miya <u>wa</u> itiya-no koto-o namakokorouku
        prince SFP one.night-GEN affair-ACC painful
        obosare
        feel.HONORIF
        'The prince felt that the affair the other night was painful.'
        (*Izumi Shikibu Nikki*)
    b. Tuki-o mite zo nisi-higasi-o <u>ba</u> siri-keru.[10]
        moon-ACC see SFP west-east-ACC SFP know-PAST
        'Looking at the moon, I found out which was west and which was east.'
        (*Tosa Nikki*)

We have not taken up the topic marker *wa* and the S-final particle *wa* in MJ, since their meanings do not seem to be the same. Various instances of *wa* in OJ given in (43)–(45), however, share the foregrounding function, suggesting that they are the same particle.

The properties of the S-final particles we have examined so far and some others can be summarized in (46).

---

[10] *Wa* is pronounced as *ba* after the accusative marker *o*.

(46)

		(i) S-final predicate	(ii) S-final non-predicate	(iii) S-internal phrase
MJ	ne	○ (17a,b)	○ (18a–c)	○ (19a–c)
	yo	○ (17a,b)	○ (18a–c)	○ (19a–c)
	sa	○ (17a,b)	○ (18a–c)	○ (19a–c)
	na	○ (17a,b)	○ (18a–c)	○ (19a–c)
	ka	○ (32a)	○ (32c)	× (32b) (○ as indefinite)
	zo	○ (36a)	× (36b)	× (36c)
	ze	○	×	×
	wa	○	×	×
OJ	ka	○ (29a,b)	○ (30a,b)	○ (31a,b)
	zo	○ (33a,b)	○ (34a,b)	○ (35a,b)
	ya	○ (37a,b)	○ (38a,b)	○ (39a,b)
	yo	○ (40a,b)	○ (41a,b)	○ (42a,b)
	wa	○ (43a,b)	○ (44)	○ (45a,b)

The first four particles in MJ and all the OJ particles in (46) allow the three usages quite consistently, which suggests that their positional versatility is not accidental but to be deduced on principled grounds. It is not obvious why some MJ particles allow usages (ii) and (iii) while others do not. One property that might be relevant to this contrast is the possible occurrence of *no* before the particles: *ne*, *yo*, *sa*, and *na* can be preceded by *no* under usage (i) and allows (ii) and (iii), while *zo*, *ze*, and *wa* show the opposite pattern. Interestingly, *no* is totally excluded in usages (ii) and (iii). We will come back to this point in Section 5.

4 S-final Particles in Other East Asian Languages

S-final particles are one of the hallmarks of East Asian languages. Some of them allow the three usages just like those in Japanese discussed in the previous sections. (47)–(49) are data from modern and Old Chinese, where (a)–(c) in each example exemplify usages (i)–(iii), respectively.[11]

---

[11] All the examples of modern Chinese are taken from *Dangdai Beijing Kouyu Yuliao: Luyin Wenben* managed by Institute of Linguistic Studies, Beijing Language and Culture University available at http://app.blcu.edu.cn/yys/6_beijing/6_beijing_chaxun.asp.

(47) Modern Chinese *Ne*
    a. yuanyi hui jia gan huor <u>ne</u>.
       want return home do housework SFP
       'I want to go home and do housework.'
    b. gei women xiao guniang kan xiaohair, zai qinghua yuanr nar <u>ne</u>.
       for our small daughter take.care child at Qinghua Garden there SFP
       'It is at Qinghua Garden there that they take care of our grandchild for our daughter.'
    c. zhexie lizi <u>ne</u> ye keyi duo jian.
       these examples SFP also possible much speak
       'As for these illustrations, you may spend much explanation.'

(48) Modern Chinese *A*
    a. haizi-men dou zai waitou gei ren bao huasheng <u>a</u>.
       child-PL all at outside for people peel peanuts SFP
       'All those children crack the shell of peanuts for other people outside.'
    b. tamen chi de dou shi baimi <u>a</u>.
       they eat DE all is white.rice SFP
       'What they eat is always white rice.'
    c. na zhi gou <u>a</u> wo yijing kan guo le.
       that CL dog SFP I already see PERF PAST
       'As for that dog, I have already seen it.'

(49) Old Chinese *Ye*
    a. zi yue bu zhi <u>ye</u>.
       master say NEG know SFP
       'Master said "I don't know".'
       (*Lunyu*)
    b. cheng ji ren <u>ye</u>, cheng wu zhi <u>ye</u>.
       complete oneself humanity SFP complete things intellect SFP
       'What completes oneself is humanity, what completes everything is intellect.'
       (*Zhongyong*)
    c. Hui <u>ye</u> wen yi yi zhi shi.
       Hui SFP hear one then understand ten
       'Hui hears one thing then understands ten things.'
       (*Lunyu*)

Modern Korean and Thai also have particles that can attach to non-predicative phrases. In particular, the polite particle *yo* in Korean can appear S-finally as well as after S-internal phrases.[12]

(50) Modern Korean *Yo*
    a. kulen-tey yo, ce nun yo mos ka-keyss-supnita yo.
       by the way SFP I TOP SFP unable go-may-POLITE SFP
       'But I am unable to go.'
       (Sohn 1999:348–350)
    b. Lee-ka yo, ecey yo, kkaphey-eyse yo, Kim-ul yo,
       Lee-NOM SFP yesterday SFP cafe-at SFP Kim-ACC SFP
       mannasse-yo.[13]
       meet-PAST SFP
       'Lee met Kim at the cafe yesterday.'
       (Dobashi and Yim 2015)

---

[12] Hiroshi Aoyagi (p.c.) points out that (50a) with *supnita* is strange and becomes perfect without it. The plural marker *tul*, which typically attaches to plural nouns, can attach to other categories (Sohn 1999:349).

(i) a. wuli meke tul poca.
       we eat TUL try
       'Let's try eating.'
    b. sinmum-ul ilk-umyense tul pap-ul mek.nunta.
       newspaper-ACC read-while TUL meal-ACC eat
       '(They) are having their meals while reading newspapers.'
    c. ppalli tul ttenala tul.
       quickly TUL leave TUL
       'Everybody, leave quickly!'
    d. nan-um ku ai tul hanthey tul chayk-ul cwu-esse.
       I-TOP the child TUL to TUL book-ACC give-PAST
       'I gave books to the children individually.'

If the second occurrence of *tul* in (ic) counts as a S-final particle, *tul* can be said to have usages (i)–(iii). According to Aoyagi, (ic) is quite strange, and *tul* does not behave like a S-final particle.

[13] Their example is slightly modified in (50b). In particular, commas are inserted after each S-internal occurrence of *yo* based on their claim that "-*yo* and [Japanese] -*ne* close off a prosodic unit as an intonational phrase." Yim (2004) argues that S-internal instances of *yo* are subject to several constraints: They are impossible without the S-final *yo*, and some manner and locative adverbs such as *tangcang* ('immediately') and *yeki* ('here') resist S-internal *yo*. Japanese S-internal usages do not obey these constraints. Yim, however, admits that manner adverbs with the particle *key* such as *sinna-key* ('with gusto') allow the S-internal *yo*.

The particle *ná* in Thai, which is often translated into *ne* in Japanese, can attach to S-final predicates as well as non-predicative phrases.[14]

(51) Modern Thai
    a. Bpai lá ná.
       go be.about.to SFP
      'I'm going.'
    b. A-rai ná?
       what SFP
      'Pardon? What was that again?'
    (Smyth 2002:152)

Besides their deictic usages, demonstrative pronouns in Vietnam can behave like S-final and interjective particles. Drawing on Cleary-Kemp (2007), Adachi (2010) argues that such usages are attested in many Malayo-Polynesian languages. In this way, the positional versatility of Japanese S-final particles discussed in Sections 2 and 3 is widely observed with S-final particles in East Asian languages.

5 S-final Particles, Scrambling, and the Lack of Agreement

The foregoing discussion has made it clear that many particles in East Asian languages exhibit the positional versatility, appearing after (i) S-final predicates, (ii) S-final non-predicates, and (iii) S-internal phrases; their properties are far from accidental and call for principled explanations.[15] In contrast, interrogative complementizers postulated in English and other European languages unambiguously attract a finite verb in the root context, as reviewed in Section 1 based on Chomsky (2008) and related work. The labeling ambiguity of locative inversion is argued to be resolved via movement, unlike that of root clauses with S-final particles. In the rest of this paper, we concentrate on Japanese and English data and attempt to shed some light into the question of why the Japanese S-final particles at stake allow multiple outputs in

---

[14] With a different tone, *ná* has S-internal usages.

(i) pôo-yĭng nǎ gôr bpen yàhng nún.
    women SFC well are like that
    'Women, right, are like that.'
    (Smyth 2002:153)

[15] A preliminary analysis of S-internal instances of S-final particles has been presented in Yasui (2014a).

the root context without inducing phrasal movement or incurring selectional violations, while English lacks analogous particles.[16] To this end, we first present a more elaborate analysis of the Japanese S-final particles sketched in Section 2.

5.1 Left-peripheral S-final Particles

Consider the three usages of the particle *ne* discussed in Section 2, which are repeated in (52a–c).

(52) a. Taro-ga   Hanako kara sakuzitu kono tegami-o morat-ta
       Taro-NOM Hanako from yesterday this letter-ACC receive-PAST
       <u>ne</u>.
       SFP
       'Taro received this letter from Hanako yesterday.'
   b. Taro-ga   sakuzitu kono tegami-o morat-ta   no-wa
      Taro-NOM yesterday this letter-ACC receive-PAST NO-TOP
      Hanako kara <u>ne</u>.
      Hanako from SF
      'It is from Hanako that Taro received this letter yesterday.'
   c. Taro-ga <u>ne</u>, Hanako-kara sakuzitu kono tegami-o morat-ta.

We have suggested the possibility of deriving (52a–c) from the same schematic structure (20a) repeated below as (53a):

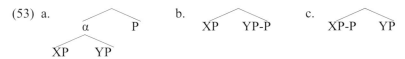

P in (53a) subsumes those particles that allow usages (i)–(iii). As has been demonstrated, they can attach not only to predicates with a tense morpheme like *ta* as in (52a), but also to nouns, case-particles, and adverbs as in (52b,c), which cannot directly take any tense or inflectional morphemes. Given the lack of selectional restrictions by the particles at stake, labeling α in (53a) in terms of either constituent should cause no selectional violations. Suppose furthermore that selection by P needs to be phonetically realized as

---

[16] Gabbo, Munaro, and Polleto (2015) discuss S-internal and S-final occurrences of particles in northern Italian dialects, which have similar discourse-level functions to those of Japanese S-final particles. They, however, occur S-initially, which is impossible in Japanese.

its suffixation onto the phrase it selects, which is reasonably attributed to its morphologically bound status. Then, we have (53b,c) from (53a). (52a,b) fall under (53b), while (52c) under (53c). The distinction in the former is that YP is a finite predicate in (52a), and a non-predicative phrase in (52b). As for the whole structure of (53a), it is trivially labeled by the S-final particle P. It follows that (53a) is a S-final particle phrase (i.e., a constituent with a certain speaker's attitude expressed on it by the particle), regardless of whether the particle is pronounced S-finally or S-internally.

If this line of analysis is on the right track, multiple outputs are obtained not only via movement plus feature agreement as in locative inversion in English but also due to the existence of morphologically bound lexical items like S-final particles that impose no selectional restrictions on the constituent they attach to.

5.2 Non-peripheral and Multiple S-final Particles

(52c) exemplifies the left-peripheral occurrence of phrases with the particle *ne*. *Ne* and the other S-final particles at stake can appear in the middle of sentences as in (54a), multiply as in (54b), and even after deeply embedded constituents as in (54c).

(54) a. Taro-ga   Hanako kara ne, sakuzitu kono tegami-o
       Taro-NOM Hanako from SFP yesterday this letter-ACC
       morat-ta.
       receive-PAST
       'Taro received this letter from Hanako yesterday.'
   b. Taro-ga ne, Hanako kara ne, sakuzitu ne, kono tegami-o ne, morat-ta yo.[17]
   c. Taro-wa [Hanako-ga   Yoshiko-ni ne, hon-o   age-ta]
       Taro-TOP Hanako-NOM Yoshiko-DAT SFP book-ACC give-PAST
       no-o   sitteiru.
       NO-ACC   know
       'Taro knows that Hanako gave the book to Yoshiko.'

(54a,b) have the same thematic meaning as that of (52c); they differ as to which part of the sentence is focused. Unlike (52c), (54a–c) do not fit into the configuration in (53c) as they are.

---

[17] *Ne* can appear multiply with S-internal phrases, but a different particle such as *yo* is more natural in S-final position as in (54b).

Setting aside (54b) for the moment, we claim that scrambling renders (54a,c) eligible for the analysis in (53c) as follows:

(55) a. Hanako kara [Taro-ga <Hanako kara> sakuzitu kono
Hanako from Taro-NOM Hanako from yesterday this
tegami-o morat-ta]
letter-ACC receive-PAST
'From Hanako, Taro received this letter yesterday.'

b. Yoshiko-ni [Taro-wa [Hanako-ga <Yoshiko-ni> hon-o
Yoshiko-DAT Taro-TOP Hanako-NOM Yoshiko-DAT book-ACC
age-ta] no-o sitteiru]
give-PAST NO-ACC know
'To Yoshiko, Taro knows that Hanako gave the book.'

The configuration of (55a,b) can be schematized as (56).

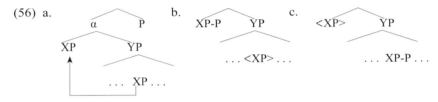

In (56a), XP is scrambled to the left-peripheral position. Without P, XP needs to be pronounced in the landing site; otherwise, scrambling would have no effects at the interfaces. With P, however, the option of pronouncing the lower copy as in (56c) should be possible since it causes no PF vacuity due to the presence of P. In other words, (56c) instantiates an in-situ option of scrambling on a par with that of *wh*-movement, which is one of the defining characteristics of Japanese. Not surprisingly, P can also be pronounced in the higher position as described in (56b); (57) is acceptable in addition to (54a).

(57) Hanako-kara ne, [Taro-ga sakuzitu kono tegami-o morat-ta]
Hanako from SFP Taro-NOM yesterday this letter-ACC receive-PAST

(54a), (55a), and (57) clearly share the thematic meaning. Moreover, *Hanako-kara* is focused in all the three examples; it is focused due to the particle in (54a), by overt scrambling in (55a), and via both means in (57).

Going back to the case of multiple S-final particles in (54b), we claim that it involves multiple scrambling like (58).

(58) kono tegami-o [sakuzitu [Hanako-kara [Taro-ga
 this   letter-ACC yesterday Hanako from   Taro-NOM
 <Hanako-kara> <sakuzitu> <kono tegami-o> morat-ta]]]
  Hanako from   yesterday   this letter-ACC receive-PAST
 Lit. 'This letter, yesterday, from Hanako, Taro received.'

The same S-final particle may not overtly appear more than once in S-final position, but certain combinations of distinct S-final particles are possible as shown below:

(59) a. Taro-ga Hanako kara sakuzitu kono tegami-o morat-ta <u>yo</u> <u>ne</u> (*<u>yo</u> <u>ne</u> <u>ne</u>).
  b. . . . morat-ta <u>yo</u> <u>na/ka</u> <u>na/ka</u> <u>ne/ka</u> <u>yo/wa</u> <u>ne/wa</u> <u>yo</u>.

If each of the bracketed constituents in (58) is selected by some S-final particle, the following configurations results.

(60)

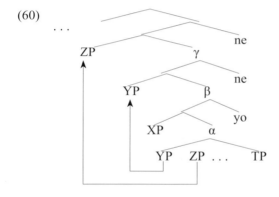

(54b) can be obtained if the lowest particle *yo* selects α and hence is morphologically affixed to its rightmost constituent, while the other particles are spelled out with internal phrases in their scrambled position. If each particle selects and is affixed to α, β, and γ, the unacceptable example in (59a) results. It seems reasonable to exclude this possibility at the PF interface; two or more instances of a single S-final particle is phonetically reduced to one, and/or no more than two particles can be phonetically realized adjacently.[18]

 One problem with this account is the island sensitivity of scrambling claimed by Saito (1985) and subsequent work. For instance, extractions out

---

[18] Our analysis predicts that internal phrases may not host more than one S-final particles, which is born out; sequences like *Taro-ga-yo-ne* and *Taro-ga-yo-na* are impossible.

of relative clauses and of a left-branch constituent are quite bad as shown in (61a) and (62a), but S-final particles can attach to the 'scrambled' phrases in their original position as illustrated in (61b) and (62b).

(61) a. *<u>Yoshiko-ni</u>   [Taro-wa   [Hanako-ga   <Yoshiko-ni>   age-ta
　　　　Yoshiko-DAT   Taro-TOP   Hanako-NOM   Yoshiko-DAT   give-PAST
　　　　hon]-o   torimodosi-ta]
　　　　book-ACC   get.back-PAST
　　　　Lit. 'To Yoshiko, Taro got back the book Hanako had given ___.'
　　b. Taro-wa   [Hanako-ga   <u>Yoshiko-ni</u>   <u>ne</u>,   age-ta   hon]-o
　　　　Taro-TOP   Hanako-NOM   Yoshiko-DAT   SFP   give-PAST   book-ACC
　　　　torimodosi-ta.
　　　　get.back-PAST

(62) a. *<u>Kono</u>   [Taro-ga   sakuzitu   Hanako   kara   <kono>   tegami-o
　　　　this   Taro-NOM   yesterday   Hanako   from   this   letter-ACC
　　　　morat-ta]
　　　　receive-PAST
　　　　Lit. 'This, Taro received ___ letter from Hanako yesterday.'
　　b. Taro-ga   sakuzitu   Hanako   kara   <u>kono</u>   <u>ne</u>,   tegami-o
　　　　Taro-NOM   yesterday   Hanako   from   this   SFP   letter-ACC
　　　　morat-ta.
　　　　receive-PAST

As is well-known and particularly mentioned by Chomsky (2013:41), structurally ambiguous and garden path sentences are often hard to interpret but are regarded as well-formed in the sense that they result from iterative applications of free Merge. If (61a) and (62a) only pause interpretive difficulties of this kind, the acceptability of (61b) and (62b) is far from surprising. We assume that scrambling as an instance of free Merge can apply unrestrictively in the computation and that the option of pronouncing a lower copy is available as far as it causes no PF vacuity.[19]

In Fukui's (1986, 1988) and Kuroda's (1988) approach to the fundamental architecture of Japanese, the lack of agreement is its defining property, from which a variety of properties that are not observed in agreement-inducing languages like English follow. If our analysis of the Japanese S-final particles is correct, their distributional versatility is closely related to the avail-

---

[19] Another potential problem is the fact that a subject can host a S-final particle. It is necessary to assume that the subject can scramble and be undone.

ability of scrambling, and ultimately to the lack of agreement in Japanese.

5.3 Disappearance of Kakarimusubi

Three of the OJ S-final particles discussed in Section 3, when affixed to S-internal phrases, required the closest predicate to be surfaced as its attributive form. This phenomenon, referred to as Kakarimusubi, has been analyzed as a kind of agreement (Ikawa 1998 and Watanabe 2004). Such analyses amount to claiming that Japanese has turned from agreement-inducing into non-agreement-inducing. Kakarimusubi, however, is quite distinct from the agreement phenomenon observed in finite clauses in English in that the latter occurs in embedded as well as root finite clauses while predicates associated with the Kakari-particles are restricted to matrix ones except in the quotative construction. Let us assume that Japanese lacked agreement-inducing morphemes in OJ just as it does now. To see if this assumption is feasible, it seems appropriate to focus on the interrogative particle *ka* in OJ since it is uncontroversial to identify it semantically with *ka* in MJ occurring in S-final position, but the latter ceased to be an interrogative marker in S-internal position as has been discussed in Section 3.

Oono (1993) offers an insightful account of this historical change. Analyzing attributive forms in OJ on a par with clauses nominalized by *no* in MJ, Oono claims that Kakarimusubi with an attributive predicate involves inversion: The constituent with the Kakari particle is its inverted predicate, and the rest of the clause ending with the attributive predicate as its logical subject. Oono illustrates the point with (63a), which is argued to be paraphrasable into (63b).

(63) a. Kurahasi-no   yama-o   takami ka, [yogomori ni idekuru
       Kurahasi-GEN mountain-ACC   height SFP late.night at coming
       tuki-no   hikari tobosiki]
       moon-GEN   light   faint
       (*Manyo-shu*:290)
       'Is it because Mt. Kurahashi is high that the light of the moon coming up late at night is weak?'
    b. [Yogomori ni idekuru tuki-no hikari tobosiki](-wa) Kurahasi-no yama-o takami ka.

(63b) is a cleft construction; the bracketed part is a nominalized clausal subject.[20] The attributive form of the predicate in (63a) in contrast to the conclusive form, which is a default choice to end a sentence, signals that what is underlyingly S-final is not the bracketed part but the preceding *ka*-marked phrase. It is then expected that OJ *ka* can type the whole structure as interrogative even if it surfaces in S-internal position.

It has been established in traditional grammar that Kakarimusubi gradually disappeared as the conclusive form was replaced by or fused with the attributed form in clause-final position. It can be argued that S-internal instances of *ka* ceased to type a clause as interrogative since nothing could indicate that they were underlyingly S-final. Instead, *ka* in S-internal position turned into an indefinite marker. *Ka* as a clause-type marker extended its distribution from roots to embedded clauses as well; *ka* is no longer a S-final particle and quite close to interrogative Cs in English and other European languages. Another interrogative marker *ya* became totally obsolete as a S-final particle. Other particles allowing the S-internal usage like *yo* have nothing to do with the interrogative/declarative distinction.[21] Their S-internal usages are innocuous since they do not type a clause.

Oono's explanation of Kakarimusubi essentially accords with our proposal. Section 2 has pointed out the parallelism between the S-internal usage of the MJ particles and the cleft construction as illustrated by (18) and (19) on a par with (63a,b). Compare (64a) with (18b), which is repeated as (64b) below.

(64) a. Hanako kara [Taro-ga   sakuzitu   kono tegami-o
       Hanako from [Taro-NOM yesterday this letter-ACC
       morat-ta]   no   ne/yo/sa/na.
       receive-PAST]   NO   SFP
       'From Hanako, Taro received this letter yesterday.'
   b. [Taro-ga   sakuzitu   kono tegami-o   morat-ta]   no-wa
       Taro-NOM   yesterday this letter-ACC receive-PAST NO-TOP
       Hanako-kara] ne/yo/sa/na.
       Hanako-from   SFP

---

[20] *Ka*, *zo*, and *namu* require the predicate to take its attributive form under usage (i), but this is not essential since no inversion is involved in that usage. In fact, *ya*, which requires the predicate to take its attributive form in the Kakarimusubi construction, requires its conclusive or realis form under usage (i).

[21] The particle *na*, which constitutes a negative imperative, cannot appear S-internally just like the interrogative *ka*.

'It is from Hanako that Taro received this letter yesterday.'

c. Kore-wa   Hanako-kara   ne/yo/sa/na.
    this-TOP Hanako-from   SFP
    'This is from Hanako.'

No in (64b) can be analyzed as converting the bracketed clause into a subject noun phrase corresponding to the demonstrative *kore* in (64c). (64a) shows that the homophonous morpheme can appear after the bracketed clause. Suppose that *no* in (64a) is the same lexical item as *no* in (64b). Then, the function of *no* in (64a) approximates the attributive form in OJ; the bracketed clause with *no* is not a finite predicate but a NP. As has been mentioned at the end of Section 3, the availability of usages (ii) and (iii) coincides with the possibility of *no* after the finite predicate under usage (i). This means that those particles that allow usages (ii) and (iii) do not require a finite predicate even under usage (i); they do not necessarily select a TP. Then, the two major constituents of (64a) corresponding to XP and YP in configuration (53a) are symmetric in that neither is necessarily a finite predicate.[22] If they are linearly switched and the particles attach to the latter constituent, we get (64b). (64b) is a cleft with the S-final particles on a par with the OJ example in (63b).

It should be noted, however, that Kakarimusubi is more restricted than S-internal usages of the MJ particles in that the phrase with a Kakari particle needs to be pronounced in left-peripheral position as pointed out by Ikawa (1998:8–10): If it is not a subject, it needs to occur to the left of the subject. In other words, the Kakari particles have to be pronounced with the higher copy as schematized in (56b), while the MJ particles can be pronounced with the scrambled phrase in its original position as in (56c), repeated as (65b,c) below.

(65)

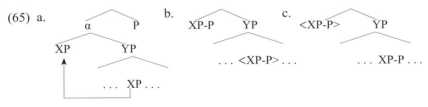

---

[22] Remember that the S-final particles in MJ in their S-internal usage can be preceded by the copula *da* but cannot by its past form *dat-ta*, which suggests that XP cannot be finite, either.

Moreover, Kakarimusubi requires the predicate of YP to take its attributive form, while no such requirement is observed with the S-internal usage of the MJ particles. We conjecture that this historical shift has to do with the disappearance of the S-internal usage of the interrogative *ka* in MJ.

One salient difference between (65b) and (65c) is that the syntactic structure given in (65a) is straightforwardly recoverable from the former; YP and the pronounced segment of XP are sisters or linearly adjacent in (65b) just as in (65a), while they are in the domination relation. If a language is a set of sound-meaning or PF-LF pairs, which should be true at least to some extent (see Chomsky 2014), and P has meaning relevant to LF, P needs to be construed at LF as having merged with the constituent consisting of XP and YP, namely α in (65a). If P has a non-syntactic or discourse-related function, its pronunciation with the lower copy should cause no interpretive difficulty at LF. *Ka* clearly needs to be interpreted as typing α in (65a), while the other MJ S-final particles do not, and hence their S-internal usages can take the option in (65c). *Ka* in OJ could function as an interrogative marker since its S-internal usage conformed to (65b).

The standard conception of agreement is that a lexical item with specific properties relates the constituent it heads with another constituent immediately dominated by its maximal projection (i.e., its specifier); the head completes its agreement function within the structure it forms. On the other hand, P in configuration (65a) behaves like an agreeing head with respect to XP and YP in that it can potentially select both due to their symmetricity, but P is outside α; P is the head of neither XP nor YP. This contrast might be a key to explaining why the standard agreement occurs in the embedded context, while the agreement-like relation triggered by a S-final particle is restricted to the root sentence.

6 Implications for the Theory of Phases: Initial and Recursive Symbol *S*

The definition of a (formal) language must include the specification of the initial symbol (see Sipser 1997). In the bottom-up conception of structure building with free Merge, the requirement can be restated as the specification of a type of syntactic objects whose generation can terminate the computation. The initial symbol in principle is not prevented from appearing to the right of the arrow in rewriting rules or before the computation terminates. In fact, the *Aspects* model recursively introduces a variant of the initial symbol to yield embedded clauses as mentioned in the introduction of this volume.

Declarative and interrogative sentences must be finite in English and other languages with overt agreement. If imperatives are also analyzed as involving some tense, it can be generalized that the initial symbol should correspond to the syntactic object labeled by a finite tense. The 'initial' or 'computation-terminating' syntactic object can become an embedded clause by merging with Cs such as *that*, *if*, [WH], and subordinate conjunctions. According to the phase-based theory of Spell-Out in Chomsky (2000, 2001) and related work, a finite embedded TP is transferred to the PF/LF interfaces when the C selecting it completes its functions. The finite embedded TP is labeled as such due to the finite T whose features are shared between the subject and the predicate it heads. Thus, the spelled-out embedded clause is labeled, independently of the C selecting it.

If a declarative sentence is also selected by some abstract C, and the phase-based Spell-Out applies strictly to it, the TP is transferred to the interfaces but the C remains in the workplace, which is not desirable. If a declarative sentence is a TP without a C, and TP is designated as the initial symbol, the whole structure, which is labeled via the agreement head T, may innocuously remain in the workplace and the computation halts properly. What about an interrogative sentence, which is standardly assumed to be a CP? We can maintain that it is also essentially a TP by assuming that T-related features like φ-features, tense, and clause-typing features originate in the T head and that nothing prevents the T from merging with its own projection, as has been proposed in the theories of extended projection (Grimshaw 1997 and Broekhuis 2013), phase extension (Dikken 2006), and phase-sliding (Gallego and Uriagereka 2006) as well as Yasui (2014a,b).[23] Interrogative matrix clauses involve the movement of T rather than the head of the subject as discussed in Section 1 simply because the feature to type a clause as interrogative originates in the matrix T.[24] If the initial symbol is TP, whether the computation continues or not depends on whether the initial symbol is selected by a C or not. If this conception of clausal architecture is on the right track, Ts and Cs play vital and interdependent roles in the computation of English and other agreement-inducing languages in that they signal the computation to halt or continue.

Does Japanese have lexical items that control the computation in the

---

[23] Yasui (2014a) argues that these features inherently appear as part of lexical items like *that*, *if*, *whether*, and modals.

[24] The fact that locative inversion is largely restricted to the matrix clause can be accounted for along the same line.

same manner? Japanese clearly has a morpheme that expresses the past tense, *ta*, and most sentences end with predicates that can host *ta*. It has been discussed in Section 2, however, that cleft sentences with S-final particles need not end with a finite predicate, as exemplified in (18) and (64). It can be said that the initial symbol of Japanese cannot simply be identified with TP. If it were TP, the root clause cannot be labeled due to the lack of φ-features in T, unlike in English. Embedded TPs are not labeled for the same reason.

As for Cs, Murasugi (1991) convincingly shows that a Japanese relative clause is not a CP but a TP. The quotative marker *to* is often analyzed as a C, but Fukui (1988) argues that it is a postposition. We can at least safely say that *to* is not a C that obligatorily selects TPs since it introduces not only full tensed clauses but also interjections like *kya* ('Eek!') and *fun* ('huh'). The absence of overt *wh*-movement is consistent with the claim that Japanese lacks a [WH] C. Many adverbial clauses are headed by nouns such as *toki* ('time'), *mae* ('front/before'), *ato* ('back/after'), and *sai* ('circumstance'), while others end with predicates in their specific conjugational forms followed by some bound morphemes. It can be said that no strong evidence supports the presence of Cs in the Japanese lexicon.

If Japanese lacks Cs and matrix clauses need not end with finite predicates, it cannot control the computation in the way English does. We speculate that Japanese and other East Asian languages have S-final particles precisely because the computation must halt where a syntactic object corresponding to a 'sentence' is produced.

References

Adachi, Mayumi. 2010. Betonamugo-no bunmatsushi: đây, này, ây, kia (Sentence-final particles in Vietnam: đây, này, ây, kia). *Tokyo Daigaku Gengogaku Ronshu* 30:1–7.
Alexiadou, Artemis and Elena Anagnostopolou. 2001. The subject-in-situ generalization and the role of case in driving computations. *Linguistic Inquiry* 32:193–231.
Bresnan, Joan. 1994. Locative inversion and the architecture of universal grammar. *Language* 70 (1):72–131.
Broekhuis, Hans. 2013. Feature inheritance versus extended projections. Ms. Meertens Institute, Amsterdam.
Chao, Yuen Ren. 1968. *A grammar of spoken Chinese*. Berkeley: University of California Press.
Chomsky, Noam. 2000. Minimalist inquiries: The framework. In *Step by step: Essays on minimalist syntax in honor of Howard Lasnik*, eds. by Roger Martin, David

Michaels, and Juan Uriagereka, 89–155. Cambridge, MA: MIT Press.
Chomsky, Noam. 2001. Derivation by phase. In *Ken Hale: A life in language*, ed. by Michael Kenstowicz, 1–52. Cambridge, MA: MIT Press.
Chomsky, Noam. 2008. On phases. In *Foundational issues in linguistic theory: Essays in honor of Jean-Roger Vergnaud*, eds. by Robert Freidin, Carlos P. Otero, and Maria Luisa Zubizarreta, 133–166. Cambridge, MA: MIT Press.
Chomsky, Norm. 2013. Problems of projection. *Lingua* 130:33–49.
Chomsky, Norm. 2014. Minimalist recursion: Exploring the prospects. In *Recursion: Complexity in cognition*, eds. by Thomas Roeper and Margaret Speas, 1–15. New York: Springer.
Chomsky, Noam. 2015. Problems of projection: Extensions. In *Structures, strategies and beyond: Studies in honour of Adriana Belletti*, eds. by Elisa Di Domenico, Cornelia Hamann, and Simona Matteini, 1–16. Amsterdam/Philadelphia: John Benjamins.
Cleary-Kemp, Nessica. 2007. Universal uses of demonstratives: Evidence from four Malayo-Polynesian languages. *Oceanic Linguistics* 46 (2):325–347.
Collins, Chris. 1997. *Local economy*. Cambridge, MA: MIT Press.
Collins, Chris and Phil Branigan. 1997. Quotative Inversion. *Natural Language and Linguistic Theory* 15:1–41.
Dikken, Marcel den. 2006. *Relators and linkers: The syntax of predication, predicate inversion, and copulas*. Cambridge, MA: MIT Press.
Dobashi, Yoshihiko and Changguk Yim. 2015. A prosodic approach to sentence-medial attachment of discourse particles in Korean and Japanese. Paper presented at the 151st Annual Meeting of the Linguistics Society of Japan, Nagoya University, 28–29 November.
Donati, Caterina. 2005. On *wh*-head-movement. In *Wh-movement moving on*, eds. by Lisa Cheng and Norbert Corver, 21–46. Cambridge, MA: MIT Press.
Emonds, Joseph. 1970. *Root and structure-preserving transformations*. Doctoral dissertation, MIT, Cambridge, MA.
Fukui, Naoki. 1986. *A theory of category projection and its applications*. Doctoral dissertation, MIT, Cambridge, MA.
Fukui, Naoki. 1988. Deriving the differences between English and Japanese: A case study in parametric syntax. *English Linguistics* 5:249–270.
Gabbo, Francesca del, Nicola Munaro, and Cecilia Polleto. 2015. On sentential particles: A crosslinguistic study. In *Final particles*, eds. by Sylvie Hancil, Alexander Haselow, and Margji Post, 359–386. Berlin: Walter de Gruyter.
Gallego, Ángel and Juan Uriagereka. 2006. Sub-extraction from subjects. Paper presented at West Coast Conference on Formal Linguistics (WCCFL) 25 and Linguistic Symposium on Romance Languages (LSRL) 36, 1 April.
Grimshaw, Jane. 1997. Projection, heads and optimality. *Linguistic Inquiry* 28:373–422.
Hoekstra, Tuen and Rene Mulder. 1990. Unergatives as copular verbs: Locational and existential predication. *The Linguistic Review* 7:1–79.
Ikawa, Hajime. 1998. On Kakarimusubi in Old Japanese: A possibility under a per-

spective of generative grammar. *Journal of Japanese Linguistics* 16:1–38.
Kuroda, Shige-Yuki. 1988. Whether we agree or not. *Linguisticae Investigationes* 12:1–47.
Masuoka, Takashi and Takubo Yukinori. 1992. *Kiso nihongo bumpo* (Basic Japanese grammar). Tokyo: Kuroshio.
Moro, Andrea. 2000. *Dynamic antisymmetry*. Cambridge, MA: MIT Press.
Murasugi, Keiko. 1991. *Noun phrases in Japanese and English: A study in syntax, learnability and acquisition*. Doctoral dissertation, The University of Connecticut, Storrs.
Oono, Susumu. 1993. *Kakarimusubi-no kenkyu* (A study of Kakarimusubi). Tokyo: Iwanami Shoten.
Richards, Marc D. 2007. On feature inheritance: An argument from the Phase Impenetrability Condition. *Linguistic Inquiry* 38:563–572.
Rizzi, Luigi and Ur Shlonsky. 2006. Satisfying the subject criterion by a nonsubject: English locative inversion and heavy NP shift. In *Phases of interpretation* ed. by Mara Frascarelli, 341–361. Berlin: Mouton de Gruyter.
Saito, Mamoru. 1985. *Some asymmetries in Japanese and their theoretical implications*. Doctoral dissertation, MIT, Cambridge, MA.
Saito, Mamoru. 2014. On the role of structural Cases in the interpretation of phrase structure. Paper presented at the Keio Institute of Cultural and Linguistic Studies, 4 September.
Sipser, Michael. 1997. *Introduction to the theory of computation*. Boston, MA: PWS Publishing.
Smyth, David. 2002. *Thai: An essential grammar*. London and New York: Routledge.
Sohn, Ho-Min. 1999. *The Korean language*. Cambridge: Cambridge University Press.
Watanabe, Akira. 2004. Loss of overt *wh*-movement in Old Japanese. In *Syntactic effects of morphological change* ed. by David W. Lightfoot, 179–195. New York: Oxford University Press.
Yasui, Miyoko. 2014a. Innocuousness of {XP, YP} as a root clause in Japanese and English. In *MIT Working Papers in Linguistics 73: Proceedings of Formal Approaches to Japanese Linguistics (FAJL) 7*, eds. by Shigeto Kawahara and Mika Igarashi, 277–288. Cambridge, MA, MIT, Graduate students in the MIT Doctoral Program in Linguistics.
Yasui, Miyoko. 2014b. Internal Head Merger and Upward Feature Sharing. Paper presented at Workshop on the Phasehood of CP and Other Projections in the 32nd Conference of the English Linguistic Society of Japan, Gakushuin University, 8 November.
Yim, Changguk. 2012. Fragment answers containing -*yo* in Korean: New evidence for the PF deletion theory of ellipsis. *Linguistic Inquiry* 43:514–518.

Island Repair and the Derivation by Phase*

Hidekazu Tanaka

> The present paper demonstrates, contrary to the standard belief, that island repair is not a general property of ellipsis: some elliptical constructions, most notably sluicing, cancel island violation, while others do not. Hence, any accounts of island repair, which presuppose that island repair is a property of ellipsis in general, must be dispensed with. Adopting the LF-copying account of island repair (Chung, Ladusaw, and McCloskey 1995), it is demonstrated that those constructions that do not permit island repair cannot be interpreted through LF-copying, which forces PF-deletion, and consequently, can result in island violations.
>
> *Keywords:* ellipsis, island repair, phase, sluicing, right-dislocation

1 Introduction

Elliptical constructions have been the focus of much interest in the recent syntactic theorizing. One reason for this is that elided constituents display a cluster of syntactic properties that are not shared by their non-elliptical counterparts. For instance, it is well-known that sluicing can ameliorate potential violations of island conditions (Chung, Ladusaw, and McCloskey 1995, Ross 1969 among many others). (1) would be ungrammatical were it not for the ellipsis of the phrase in angled brackets.

(1) They are looking for someone who speaks a Balkan language, but I don't know which (Balkan language) <*they are looking for someone who speaks t>.

Similarly, (2) and (3) violate the coordinate structure constraint and the subject condition, respectively, and would remain ungrammatical without ellipsis

---

* The materials reported here are a revised version of the paper presented at International Linguistics Workshop at Dokkyo University. I would like to thank the audience at the workshop, especially Jun Abe, Željko Bošković, and Miyoko Yasui. The author alone is responsible for any shortcomings that may be found herein.

(Ross 1967).

(2) Irv and someone were dancing together, but I don't know who <*Irv and t were dancing together>.

(3) That he'll hire someone is possible, but I won't divulge who <*that he'll hire t is possible>.

Since Ross (1969), the phenomenon, dubbed island repair, has received much attention, and various accounts have been offered to duly capture the phenomenon within the syntactic framework. The interest in this phenomenon, it seems, arises because the familiar poverty of stimulus argument tells us that such properties unique to elliptical constructions gives us a clue to the nature of universal grammar, since they cannot be acquired through being exposed to the initial linguistic data. After all, when a phrase is elliptical, its syntax is not directly accessible for acquisition as part of the primary linguistic data. We would therefore expect that a proper account of such facts would have non-trivial consequences to the over-all organization of syntax. This paper adds a momentum to the research in this area, by bringing in an issue that has been ignored.

While island repair is studied fairly well in the literature, what is less understood, or remains mostly unnoticed, is that some elliptical constructions cancel island violations while others do not, as discussed extensively below. This raises a question as to why this is so. Our explanation of island repair appeals to LF-copying (Chung, Ladusaw, and McCloskey 1995) for reasons that will be discussed extensively. We will critically examine two other accounts of island repair proposed in the literature.

Our proposal appeals in part to the phase theory (Chomsky 2008). The basic idea is that at the completion of each phase, the complement of the phase head is transferred to the interface levels, and hence, becomes inaccessible for the computational system. Since C and v, which head a propositional content, are the phrase heads, their complement, TP and VP, gets transferred to the interface levels, the articulatory-perceptual (AP) and conceptual-intention (CI) systems, as depicted below.

(4)

We claim that when phrases are transferred, they cannot be accessible for further computation (Phase Impenetrability Condition), but transferred phrase complements, but no other phrases, are available at the interfaces for copying. Hence, only phase complements can be copied at LF.

The rest of this paper is organized as follows: sections two and three show that island repair takes place only in a proper subset of elliptical constructions both in English and Japanese. Furthermore, the same sections also show that the two languages draw the same distinction: in order for island violations to be repaired, the antecedent TP must have a correlate phrase coreferential with the remnant phrase. Section four develops our account of the observations. We assume that elliptical phrases can be recovered, for interpretive purposes, either through LF-copying or PF-deletion. Island repair, we argue, takes place due to LF-copying, assuming that subjacency is a condition on derivation: when a phrase does not move out of the offending island, there cannot be a subjacency violation (Chung, Ladusaw, and McCloskey 1995). We argue that a phrase can only be copied at LF if it has already been transferred to the LF component. Hence, only an elliptical TP (and VP) can be interpreted through LF-copying. All other instances of ellipsis must be derived via PF-deletion, and hence, subjacency is at work throughout the derivation, which entails that there is no island repair for such elliptical constructions. The proposal gives a natural explanation to otherwise puzzling facts. Section five concludes the paper by giving a brief summary.

2 Non-Repairing Constructions in English

This section and the next list up ellipsis phenomena that do not cancel island violations. Our list consists of data from English, putting off our discussion on Japanese facts until section three. The point to be established is that, in English, there exist some elliptical constructions, like sluicing, that permit island repair, and there also exist some elliptical constructions that fail to permit island repair, showing that the distinction between the two types of elliptical constructions does not stem from parameter settings.

2.1 Sprouting

The first syntactic environment on our list is sprouting, which does not have a correlate phrase in the antecedent clause (Chung, Ladusaw, and McCloskey 1995). The *run-of-the-mill* example of sprouting is given below.

(5)   They were firing, but [at what <they were firing t>] was unclear.

(6) He finished on time, but with whose help <he finished on time t>?

These examples are to be compared against their sluicing counterparts in (7) and (8), which do have an indefinite correlate phrase in the antecedent clause.

(7) They were firing at something, but [at what <they were firing t>] was unclear.

(8) He finished on time with someone's help, but with whose help <he finished on time t>?

Sprouting observes island conditions. Examples in (9) and (10) show that sprouting fails to repair the *wh*-island condition and the subject condition, respectively (Chung, Ladusaw, and McCloskey 1995).

(9) *Agnes wondered how John could eat, but it's not clear what <Agnes wondered *how John could eat t_*>.

(10) *That Tom would win is likely, but I am not sure which race <*that Tom would win t is likely*>.

These examples contrast with their sluicing counterparts, which display island repair. Hence, (11) and (12) are grammatical in clear contrast with (9) and (10).

(11) Agnes wondered how John could eat something, but it's not clear what <Agnes wondered *how John could eat t_*>.

(12) That Tom would win a race is likely, but I am not sure which race <*that Tom would win t is likely*>.

The grammaticality contrast demands an explanation, but was left unaccounted for in Chung, Ladusaw, and McCloskey (1995). As far as I am aware, most of the recent literatures on ellipsis fail to take this into account. Nonetheless, the contrast is an important one, and as shown in the reminder of this section, the contrast obtains in much wider context than simply between sprouting and sluicing. Another non-repairing case arises when the correlate phrase in the antecedent clause contrasts with the remnant phrase, as we now see.

2.2 Wh-else: *Contrastive Focus*

In sluicing constructions, the correlate phrase in the antecedent clause does not have to be an indefinite phrase: when the remnant *wh*-phrase is accompanied by *else*, the correlate phrase can be an R-expression bearing contrastive focus intonation. (13) illustrates this point, where the capitalized phrase bear contrastive stress.

(13) HARRY came, but I don't know who else <t came>.

Let us call such sentences contrastive *else* sluicing. One interesting fact about contrastive *else* sluicing is that it cannot cancel island violations (Fox and Lasnik 2003). (14) and (15) violate the subject condition and the complex NP constraint, respectively.

(14) *That HARRY came is unfortunate, but I don't know who else <*that t came* is unfortunate>.

(15) *The detective ruled out the possibility that Fred killed ABBY, but I don't know who else <the detective ruled out *the possibility that Fred killed t*>.

Thus, contrastive *else* sluicing leagues with sprouting, as opposed to the standard sluicing, in that it cannot cancel island violations.

2.3 Adjunct Wh-*Phrases*

Huang (1982) notes that the extraction of an adjunct phrase out of a syntactic island gives rise to a notably worse result than the extraction of an argument. Thus, (16), in which an adjunct *wh*-phrase is extracted out of a *wh*-island, is considerably more grammatical than (17), in which an adjunct is extracted out of the same island.

(16) ??What$_i$ do you wonder [whether Mary destroyed t$_i$]?

(17) *Why$_i$ do you wonder [whether Mary destroyed the official document t$_i$]?

Huang explains the contrast in terms of the empty category principle (ECP), proposed in Chomsky (1981). Simply put, traces of an adjunct phrase must satisfy an additional requirement, which does not apply to argument traces, that they bear a local relation with their antecedent phrase, but island configuration blocks the local relation. (17) therefore violates the ECP.

The asymmetry has received different treatments throughout the development of syntactic theory, but we shall not be concerned with them in this paper. What is interesting for our current purpose is that adjunct island violations, traditionally attributed to the ECP (Huang 1982), cannot be wiped out through ellipsis (Sauerland 1997). This point is shown by (18).

(18) John has written a paper that proves Fermat's last theorem in the simplest possible way. *Guess how <John has found *a paper that proves Fermat's last theorem* t>.

Thus, sluicing with a remnant adjunct *wh*-phrase should be grouped together with sprouting and contrastive *else* sluicing, discussed above.

Cases we have seen so far of elliptical constructions that do not ameliorate island violations all involve ellipsis of a TP. The next section shows that VP-ellipsis does not cancel island violations, either.

2.4 Antecedent Contained Deletion (ACD)

Above sections have shown that there are cases of TP-ellipsis that do not cancel island violations. Those cases are all similar to sluicing, which involves a remnant phrase that appears to be extracted out of an elliptical TP. It is therefore easy to determine whether the remnant *wh*-phrase can cause island violation. The situation is not quite as simple for VP-ellipsis, since a typical case of VP-ellipsis does not involve extraction. For example, one cannot ask whether (19) observes island conditions, since there is no phrase that get extracted from the elliptical site to begin with.

(19) John read a report on the accident. Tom did <read a report on the accident>, too.

The case we are interested in, thus, must have a phrase that moves out of an elliptical VP. One such case of VP-ellipsis is antecedent contained deletion (ACD) constructions, since a relative operator, Op in (20), moves out of the elliptical VP.

(20) John read every report Op_i that Tom did <read t_i>.

We are therefore able to ask, based on ACD, whether VP-ellipsis can cancel island violations.

The well-known puzzle that ACD constructions pose is that the elliptical constituent is properly contained in its own antecedent. Thus, simply copying the antecedent VP to the ellipsis site causes infinite regress, as in (21).

(21) John read every report Op_i that Tom [read a report that Tom [read a report ...]].

Basically the same problem arises for the PF-deletion approach to ellipsis. In order for the elliptical VP to be identical with the antecedent VP_A, the elliptical VP_E in (22) must be identical to VP_A, but VP_A itself contains VP_E, which means that the derivational source prior to ellipsis must be infinitely long.

(22) John [$_{VPA}$ read every report Op$_i$ that Tom did <$_{VPE}$ f>].

Thus, exactly the same problem arises in ACD no matter which approach to ellipsis we take.

The standard solution of this puzzle is that this problem is resolved by quantifier raising (QR) (Kennedy 1997, May 1985, Tanaka 2011a).

(23) [every report that Tom did <$_{VPE}$ read t>]$_i$ John [$_{VPA}$ read t$_i$]
            QUANTIFIER RAISING

One good argument for the QR account is object contained ACD sentences, which call for the QR account (Kennedy 1997). Consider (24), which has a quantifier with ACD within the object noun phrase.

(24) John read a report on [$_{QP}$ every accident that Tom did <$_{VPE}$ read a report on t>].

(24), for instance, gets properly interpreted if the quantifier raises out of the object phrase, giving rise to the antecedent VP, VP$_A$ in (25). Note that the interpretation of the elliptical phrase in (25) is *read a report on*. To obtain this within the antecedent, the quantifier must raise out of the object.

(25) [every accident that Tom did <$_{VPE}$ read a report on t>]$_i$ John [$_{VPA}$ read a report on t$_i$]

What is interesting for our purpose is that the relative clause contained in the object must be well-formed. (24) contrasts with (26).

(26) *John visited a city near every lake Op$_i$ that Tom did <visited a city near t$_i$>.

The contrast arises, we argue, because of the well-formedness of the relative clauses. (24) has the well-formed relative clause in (27), while the ungrammatical (26) contains the ill-formed relative clause in (28).

(27) every accident that Tom read a report on

(28) *every lake that Tom visited a city near

The contrast can be attributed to the adjunct condition. The PP headed by *on* in (27) is a complement of the noun head *report*, while the PP headed by *near* in (28) is an adjunct, adjoined to *city*. The contrast therefore gets a natural explanation in terms of the adjunct condition. Note, however, that our account relies on the assumption that the ungrammaticality of (26) is not canceled through the application of antecedent contained deletion in (25). Thus, the ungrammaticality of (26) points to the conclusion that VP-deletion in ACD constructions cannot repair locality violations, in this case, the adjunct condition.

One possible objection here is that examples like (24) and (26) are derived through at least two different applications of A'-movement. One of them is movement of the relative operator. The other is quantifier raising (QR). One possible alternative to our account therefore is to attribute the ungrammaticality of (26) to the impossibility of QR in this syntactic context. If QR is barred in (26), there is no reason to appeal to the possibility of relative operator movement in order to account for (26). However, the contrast between (24) and (26) cannot be explained away in terms of the possibility of QR, since QR itself can freely apply in the same context. (29) and (30) show that inverse scope is possible in the same syntax context as (26).

(29) John visited a city near every lake. (every > city)

(30) Someone visited a city near every lake. (some > every, every > some)

This shows that the ungrammaticality of (26) cannot be attributed to the impossibility of QR out of an adjunct phrase. Thus, the subjacency violation in (26) is incurred by movement of the relative operator, and island repair under ellipsis fails to obtain in (26). We have thus far seen various instances of ellipsis in English that fail to repair island violations. We now turn our attention to Japanese data.

3 Right-Dislocation in Japanese

Thus far, we have seen cases of ellipsis that fail to repair island violations. All our examples come from English. This section shows that the same fact, some ellipsis repairs island violations while others do not, is also observed in Japanese, showing the cross-linguistic validity of our observation.

3.1 The Scrambling and Deletion Account

Our argument in this section is based on right-dislocation constructions Tanaka (1996). Japanese is a SOV language with a rather strict requirement that the verb appears in the sentence final position, especially in written style of the language. (32), which has an accusative phrase appearing in the post-verbal position, or (33), whose nominative subject appears in the post-verbal position, is therefore ungrammatical in clear contrast with (31), which has the canonical SOV order.

(31) Yamada-sensei-ga   Hanako-o   sikatta.
Yamada-teacher-NOM Hanako-ACC scolded
'Professor Yamada scolded Hanako.'

(32) *Yamada-sensei-ga sikatta Hanako-o.

(33) *Hanako-o sikatta Yamada-sensei-ga

Nonetheless, in a colloquial style, a constituent may appear post-verbally. Such sentences are called right-dislocation (henceforth RD). Examples like (34) and (35) frequently pop up in daily conversations. The particle -*yo* indicates that the sentence is in colloquial style, a natural context for RD sentences. RD sentences normally has a comma intonation break between the particle -*yo* and the dislocated constituent.

(34) Hanako-o   sikatta-yo, Yamada-sensei-ga.
Hanako-ACC scolded   Yamada teacher-NOM
'He scolded Hanako, Professor Yamada.'

(35) Yamada-sensei-ga   sikatta-yo, Hanako-o.
Yamada teacher-NOM scolded   Hanako-ACC
'Professor Yamada scolded her, Hanako.'

The dislocated constituent, it appears, has not undergone rightward movement, because RD is not clause-bound. This point is shown by (36) and (37). (36) has an embedded clause. An accusative object dislocates out of the complement clause to the sentence final position in (37).

(36) Taroo-ga   [Yamada-sensei-ga   Hanako-o   sikatta-to]
Taroo- NOM   Yamada teacher-NOM Hanako-ACC scolded-COMP
omotteiru.
think
'Taroo thinks that Professor Yamada scolded Hanako.'

(37) Taroo-ga   [Yamada-sensei-ga   sikatta-to]   omotteiru-yo,
Taroo- NOM   Yamada teacher- NOM scolded- COMP think
Hanako-o.
Hanako-acc
'Taroo thinks that Professor Yamada scolded her, Hanako.'

To the extent that we can determine, it is very difficult to construct an argument that Japanese observes the so-called the right-roof constraint (Ross 1967), which prohibits a phrase that moves rightward from crossing a clause boundary. At least in English, there is solid evidence that rightward movement, including extraposition, cannot take place across a clause boundary. (38) is grammatical since the extraposed phrase stays within the local clause, that is, within the sentential subject. (39) is ungrammatical because the extraposed phrase moves out of the sentential subject all the way to the matrix clause, in violation of the right-roof constraint.

(38)　[That a review came out yesterday of this article] is catastrophic.

(39)　*[[That a review came out yesterday] is catastrophic] of this article.

Given the absence of negative evidence in language acquisition, the right-roof constraint cannot be learnt through being exposed to the primary linguistic experience. We are then forced to assume that the right-roof constraint is universal. Thus, one may conclude that RD in Japanese, being free from the right-roof constraint, does not involve movement, but is derived via some movement operations, such as base-generation of the RD constituent and binding. This conjecture runs into a difficulty, because RD constructions in Japanese are subject to locality conditions, that is, island conditions (Tanaka 2001). For example, (40) violates the complex NP constraint.

(40)　*Taroo-ga　　[Yamada-sensei-ga　　sikatta　toyuu uwasa-o]
　　　 Taroo-NOM　Yamada-teacher-NOM　scolded that　 rumor-ACC
　　　 kinisiteru-yo,　　Hanako-o.
　　　 is worried about　Hanako-ACC
　　　 'Taroo is worried about the rumor that professor Yamada scolded, Hanako.'

Why is it that RD is free from the right-roof constraint but is still subject to island conditions? Tanaka (2001) offers a simple solution for this question: RD is derived via leftward movement and therefore is free from the right-roof constraint. The basic idea is that RD sentences simply repeat the root clause twice. The second root clause has the dislocated constituent scrambled to the initial position of the root clause, with the rest of the second sentence deleted under identity with the TP_A in the first clause. Such a derivation is depicted in (41).

(41)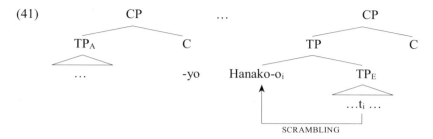

Given this account, we can conclude that scrambling in (40) violates the complex NP constraint within the ellipsis site in the second clause, as schematized below.

(42)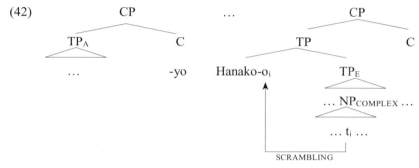

Implicit in this account is the assumption that scrambling is subject to the complex NP constraint. This well-established point is shown by (43) (Harada 1977, Saito 1985).

(43) *Taroo-ga [Yamada-sensei-ga sikatta toyuu uwasa-o]
Taroo-NOM Yamada-teacher-NOM scolded that rumor-ACC
kinisiteru-yo, Hanako-o.
is worried about Hanako-ACC
'Taroo is worried about the rumor that Professor Yamada scolded, Hanako.'

The ungrammaticality of (40), therefore, is to be attributed to the violation of the complex NP constraint in (43) that takes place within the elliptical TP.

The account sketched above seems to work well and is intuitively appealing, but faces an obvious obstacle. More specifically, the proposed account presupposes that the island violation in (40)/(42) does not get cancelled even after deletion, unlike what happens in English sluicing, which does cancel island violations. As we have seen above, eliding the TP in angled brackets cancels the complex NP constraint violation that takes place within the ellipsis site.

(44) They are looking for someone who speaks a Balkan language, but I don't know which (Balkan language) <*they are looking for someone who speaks t>.

Such a problem is overlooked in Tanaka (2001), but we are now in a position to address the problem against our cross-linguistic data: we have seen various cases in English whose island violations do not get canceled even after deletion. The observation we have in Japanese therefore opens up the possibility that the same is true in Japanese: RD in Japanese patterns with spouting, contrastive *else* sluicing, the adjunct sluicing, and antecedent contained deletion in that these instances of ellipsis cannot cancel island violations. Before developing the account of such selective island repair phenomena, it is worthwhile to go further: Japanese also has various cases of ellipsis, like English, which do not cancel island violations. At the same time, Japanese also has various cases of ellipsis, like English, which do cancel island violations. Thus, Japanese and English are parallel to each other in this respect.

3.2 Island Canceling Right Dislocation

Above, we have seen that right dislocation (RD) in Japanese fails to cancel island violations, on par with English spouting, contrastive *else* sluicing, the adjunct sluicing, and antecedent contained deletion. English also has a case of ellipsis that cancels island violations, that is, sluicing. We expect that properties of ellipsis is universal. If our reasoning is on the right track, we expect to find cases of ellipsis in Japanese, like English sluicing, that can cancel island violations. This expectation is in fact full-filled. Consider (45), a case of RD whose antecedent clause has a correlate phrase.

(45) Yamada-sensei-ga   ano-gakusei$_i$-o   sikatta-yo, Hanako-o$_i$.
Yamada-teacher-NOM that student-ACC scolded   Hanako-ACC
'Professor Yamada scolded that student, Hanako.'

In (45), the correlate phrase has a distal demonstrative marker, *ano* and its referent is supplied from the memory mutually understood between the speaker and the hearer.[1] Let us refer to those RD sentences with a correlate phrase as sluicing RD constructions, as oppose to sprouting RD, given an obvious parallel between these constructions and English sluicing and sprouting. Notice now that sluicing RD constructions, unlike their sprouting counterparts (40), repair island violations. This point is shown by (46), which has a correlate phrase within the complex NP.

(46) Taroo-ga [Yamada-sensei-ga ano-gakusei$_i$-o sikatta toyuu
Taroo-NOM Yamada-teacher-NOM the student-ACC scolded that
uwasa-o] kinisiteru-yo, Hanako-o$_i$.
rumor-ACC is worried about Hanako-ACC
'Taroo is worried about the rumor that Professor Yamada scolded that student, Hanako.'

The same point is established by (47), which, superficially, violates the adjunct condition.

(47) Taroo-ga [Yamada-sensei-ga ano-gakusei$_i$-o sikatta atode]
Taroo-NOM Yamada-teacher-NOM the student-ACC scolded after
daigaku-ni itta-yo, Hanako-o$_i$.
university-to went Hanako-ACC
'Taroo went to the university after Professor Yamada scolded that student, Hanako.'

As expected, the sluicing RD counterpart of (47) observes the adjunct condition. (48), which forms a minimal pair with (47) in that the former does not have a distal demonstrative correlate phrase within the antecedent, sharply contrasts in grammaticality with (47).

(48) *Taroo-ga [Yamada-sensei-ga sikatta atode]
Taroo-NOM Yamada-teacher-NOM scolded after
daigaku-ni itta-yo, Hanako-o$_i$.
university-to went Hanako-ACC
'Taroo went to the university after Professor Yamada scolded (her), Hanako.'

---

[1] Japanese demonstratives have three-way distinctions. *Kono* is proximal to the speaker, *sono* is proximal to the hearer, and *ano* is distal to both the speaker and the hearer. All these demonstratives, when they appear in RD constructions, can cancel island violations but examples are omitted for the former two.

Thus, sluicing RD constructions and sprouting RD constructions mirror the English contrast between sluicing and sprouting. That is, sluicing RD constructions in Japanese and sluicing in English cancel island violations, but sprouting RD constructions in Japanese and sprouting in English fail to do so. What this shows is that our observation that some instances ellipsis salvages island violations while others do not holds true across languages. Moreover, the presence of a correlate phrase, or lack thereof, is crucial in both of the languages, which calls for an explanation. Before taking on the task, we examine different manifestations of RD sentences in Japanese to sort them out.

3.3 Full-Fledged Antecedents

One argument for the repetition and ellipsis account of RD constructions listed in Tanaka (2001) is that RD constructions can have a full-fledged sentence in the antecedent. Examples below have a correlate phrase identical to the dislocated constituent.

(49) Yamada-sensei-ga   Hanako-o   sikatta-yo, Yamada-sensei-ga.
Yamada teacher-NOM Hanako-ACC scolded   Yamada teacher-NOM
'Professor Yamada scolded Hanako, Professor Yamada.'

(50) Yamada-sensei-ga   Hanako-o   sikatta-yo, Hanako-o.
Yamada teacher-NOM Hanako-ACC scolded   Hanako-ACC
'Professor Yamada scolded Hanako, Hanako.'

This type of RD constructions also cancels island violations. (43), repeated in (51), contrasts in grammaticality with (52).

(51) *Taroo-ga   [Yamada-sensei-ga   sikatta   toyuu   uwasa-o]
Taroo-NOM   Yamada-teacher-NOM   scolded   that   rumor-ACC
kinisiteru-yo,   Hanako-o.
is worried about   Hanako-ACC
'Taroo is worried about the rumor that Professor Yamada scolded, Hanako.'

(52) Taroo-ga   [Yamada-sensei-ga   Hanako-o   sikatta   toyuu
Taroo-NOM   Yamada-teacher-NOM   Hanako-ACC   scolded   that
uwasa-o]   kinisiteru-yo,   Hanako-o.
rumor-ACC   is worried about   Hanako-ACC
'Taroo is worried about the rumor that Professor Yamada scolded Hanako, Hanako.'

What these examples show is that the correlate phrase must either bear the same index as the dislocated constituent, as in (46), or be identical to the correlate phrase, as in (52), to cancel island violations. From this viewpoint, it is interesting to see if other kinds of coreferential expressions can be the correlate phrase. RD is also possible when the antecedent clause has a pronoun coreferential with the dislocated constituent, as shown by (53).

(53) Yamada-sensei-ga   kanojo$_i$-o sikatta-yo, Hanako$_i$-o.
    Yamada teacher-NOM her   scolded   Hanako-ACC
    'Professor Yamada scolded her$_i$, Hanako$_i$.'

Island repair also takes place in such a case, as (54) shows.

(54) Taroo-ga   [Yamada-sensei-ga   kanojo$_i$-o sikatta   toyuu
    Taroo-NOM Yamada-teacher-NOM   her   scolded that
    uwasa-o]   kinisiteru-yo,   Hanako$_i$-o.
    rumor-ACC   is worried about   Hanako-ACC
    'Taroo is worried about the rumor that Professor Yamada scolded her$_i$, Hanako$_i$.'

To summarize, the correlate phrase in RD constructions must be a demonstrative co-indexed with the RD constituent (46), identical to the RD constituent (52), or a pronoun coindexed with the RD constituent (54) in order to cancel island violations. All these cases point to the conclusion that RD constructions can cancel island violations when the correlate phrase is coindexed with the RD constituent. We would then expect that when the correlate phrase is not coreferential with the RD constituent, island repair fails to obtain. This expectation is borne out, as the subsequent sections show.

3.4 Non-Matching Correlate Phrases

The dislocated constituent in RD can also be non-coreferential with the correlate phrase in the antecedent. (55) and (56) illustrate such a case.

(55) Yamada-sensei-ga   Hanako-o   sikatta-yo, Sato-sensei-mo.
    Yamada teacher-NOM   Hanako-ACC scolded   Sato teacher-also
    'Professor Yamada scolded Hanako, Professor Sato (also scolded Hanako).'

(56) Yamada-sensei-ga   Hanako-o   sikatta-yo, Yoshiko-mo.
    Yamada teacher-NOM   Hanako-ACC   scolded   Yoshiko-ACC
    'Professor Yamada scolded Hanako, and also (he also scolded) Yoshiko.'

Let us refer to this kind of RD sentences as *also*-RD, since the dislocated constituent is marked with the particle *-mo* (for *also*). (57) shows that *also*-RD sentences can take place long-distance out of the complement clause.

(57) Taroo-ga   [Yamada-sensei-ga   Hanako-o   sikatta-to]
     Taroo-NOM Yamada teacher-NOM   Hanako-ACC   scolded-COMP
     omotteiru-yo, Yoshiko-mo.
     think   Yoshiko-ACC
     'Taroo thinks that Professor Yamada scolded Hanako, and also (Taroo also thinks that Professor Yamada scolded) Yoshiko.'

The fact that *also*-RD is possible out of a complement clause leads to the question as to whether extraction out of an island is possible in such a sentence. The ungrammatical examples in (58) and (59) violate the complex NP constraint, showing that *also*-RD fails to repair island violations.

(58) *Taroo-ga   [Yamada-sensei-ga   Hanako-o   sikatta   toyuu
      Taroo-NOM Yamada-teacher-NOM   Hanako-ACC   scolded   that
      uwasa-o]   kinisiteru-yo,   Sato-sensei-mo.
      rumor-ACC is worried about   Sato teacher-also
      'Taroo is worried about the rumor that Professor Yamada scolded Hanako, (he is also worried about the rumor that) Professor Sato (also scolded Hanako).'

(59) *Taroo-ga   [Yamada-sensei-ga   Hanako-o   sikatta   toyuu
      Taroo-NOM Yamada-teacher-NOM   Hanako-ACC   scolded   that
      uwasa-o]   kinisiteru-yo,   Yoshiko-mo.
      rumor-ACC is worried about   Yoshiko-also
      'Taroo is worried about the rumor that Professor Yamada scolded Hanako, (he is also worried about the rumor that Professor Yamada also scolded) Yoshiko.'

There is an obvious parallel between this case and contrastive *else* sluicing in English discussed in section 2.2, a representative example is repeated below.

(60) HARRY came, but I don't know who else <t came>.

As shown above, Fox and Lasnik (2003) point out that contrastive *else* sluicing observes island constraints.

(61) *That HARRY came is unfortunate, but I don't know who else <*that t came* is unfortunate>.

(62) *The detective ruled out the possibility that Fred killed ABBY, but I don't know who else <the detective ruled out *the possibility that Fred killed t*>.

What they have in common is that the correlate phrase do not bear the same index as the remnant phrase, and they are subject to island conditions.

3.5 Adjunct Right-Dislocation

(63) shows that adjunct phrases can undergo RD.

(63) Yamada-sensei-ga Hanako-o sikatta-yo, oogoe-de.
Yamada teacher-NOM Hanako-ACC scolded loudly
'Professor Yamada scolded Hanako, loudly.'

It is also possible for an adjunct phrase to be dislocated out of a complement clause, as (64) shows.

(64) Taroo-ga [Yamada-sensei-ga Hanako-o sikatta-to]
Taroo-NOM Yamada-teacher-NOM Hanako-ACC scolded-that
omotteiru-yo, oogoe-de
think   loudly
'Taroo thinks that Professor Yamada scolded Hanako, loudly.'

We have seen that adjunct sluicing in English observes island conditions. The crucial example is repeated here.

(65) John has written a paper that proves Fermat's last theorem in the simplest possible way. *Guess how <John has found *a paper that proves Fermat's last theorem t*>.

Given the similarities between English sluicing and Japanese RD, we would expect that adjunct RD constructions also observe island conditions. The expectation is indeed borne out. (66) does not have the interpretation whereby the dislocated adjunct phrase modifies the embedded clause within the complex NP.

(66) *Taroo-ga [Yamada-sensei-ga Hanako-o sikatta toyuu
Taroo-NOM Yamada-teacher-NOM Hanako-ACC scolded that
uwasa-o] kinisiteru-yo, oogoe-de.
rumor-ACC is worried about loudly
'Taroo is worried about the rumor that Professor Yamada scolded Hanako, loudly.'

Thus, adjunct RD constructions cannot repair island violations, on par with English adjunct sluicing.

3.6 Island Repair or Not

To summarize our discussion so far, English sluicing in (67) and those instances of Japanese RD constructions that have a coreferential correlate phrase, a distal demonstrative marker in (68), a full-fledged copy of the dislocated phrase in (69), or a pronoun coreferential with the remnant phrase (70), suffice to ameliorate island violations.

(67) They are looking for someone who speaks a Balkan language, but I don't know which (Balkan language) <*they are looking for someone who speaks t>.

(68) Taroo-ga   [Yamada-sensei-ga   ano-gakusei$_i$-o   sikatta toyuu
     Taroo-NOM Yamada-teacher-NOM the student-ACC   scolded that
     uwasa-o]   kinisiteru-yo,   Hanako-o$_i$.
     rumor-ACC is worried about   Hanako-ACC
     'Taroo is worried about the rumor that Professor Yamada scolded the student, Hanako.'

(69) Taroo-ga   [Yamada-sensei-ga   Hanako-o   sikatta toyuu
     Taroo-NOM Yamada-teacher-NOM Hanako-ACC scolded that
     uwasa-o]   kinisiteru-yo,   Hanako-o.
     rumor-ACC is worried about   Hanako-ACC
     'Taroo is worried about the rumor that Professor Yamada scolded Hanako, Hanako.'

(70) Taroo-ga   [Yamada-sensei-ga   kanojo$_i$-o   sikatta toyuu
     Taroo-NOM Yamada-teacher-NOM her   scolded that
     uwasa-o]   kinisiteru-yo,   Hanako$_i$-o.
     rumor-ACC is worried about   Hanako-ACC
     'Taroo is worried about the rumor that Professor Yamada scolded her$_i$, Hanako$_i$.'

It is clear that these have features in common. In all these instances of ellipsis, island repair takes place. The antecedent clause has either an indefinite phrase, whose index value is not fixed as in (67), or the correlate phrase in the antecedent is coreferential with the remnant phrase, as depicted in (71).

(71)

In contrast, English sprouting in (72), contrastive *else* sluicing in (73), adjunct sluicing in (74), antecedent contained deletion in (75), and those instances of Japanese RD constructions that have no correlate phrase in the antecedent in (76), or those that have contra-indexed correlate phrase in (77), and the adjunct RD sentence in (78) cannot fix island violations through ellipsis.

(72) *Agnes wondered how John could eat, but it's not clear what <Agnes wondered *how John could eat t* >.

(73) *The detective ruled out the possibility that Fred killed ABBY, but I don't know who else <the detective ruled out *the possibility that Fred killed t*>.

(74) John has written a paper that proves Fermat's last theorem in the simplest possible way. *Guess how <John has found *a paper that proves Fermat's last theorem t*>.

(75) *John visited a city near every lake Op_i that Tom did < visited a city near t_i>.

(76) *Taroo-ga [Yamada-sensei-ga sikatta toyuu uwasa-o]
Taroo-NOM Yamada-teacher-NOM scolded that rumor-ACC
kinisiteru-yo, Hanako-o.
is worried about Hanako-ACC
'Taroo is worried about the rumor that Professor Yamada scolded, Hanako.'

(77) *Taroo-ga [Yamada-sensei-ga Hanako-o sikatta toyuu
Taroo-NOM Yamada-teacher-NOM Hanako-ACC scolded that
uwasa-o] kinisiteru-yo, Yoshiko-mo.
rumor-ACC is worried about Yoshiko-also
'Taroo is worried about the rumor that Professor Yamada scolded Hanako, (he is also worried about the rumor that Professor Yamada also scolded) Yoshiko.'

(78) *Taroo-ga   [Yamada-sensei-ga   Hanako-o   sikatta   toyuu
     Taroo-NOM   Yamada-teacher-NOM   Hanako-ACC   scolded   that
     uwasa-o]   kinisiteru-yo,   oogoe-de.
     rumor-ACC   is worried about   loudly
     'Taroo is worried about the rumor that Professor Yamada scolded
     Hanako, loudly.'

Most instances of ellipsis in this set fail to have a correlate phrase coreferential with the remnant phrase, so that once copied to the ellipsis site, the remnant phrase has no variable to bind.

One clearly distinctive case is the antecedent contained deletion, which has a variable, left behind by QR, to be bound by the relative operator as schematized in (79).

(79) [every lake Op$_i$ that Tom did <$_{VPE}$ visited a city near t$_i$>]$_i$ [John [$_{VPE}$ visited a city near t$_i$]]

The empirical generalizations to be captured are summarized here.

(80) Island repair takes place when the antecedent TP contains an indefinite phrase or a correlate phrase coreferential with the remnant/dislocated phrase. When there is no coreferential correlate phrase, island repair fails to take place.

(81) VP-deletion in ACD cannot repair island violations even in the presence of a co-indexed variable in the antecedent.

What is noteworthy is the fact that our observation that island repair takes place only in a proper subset of elliptical constructions holds cross-linguistically. To account for our generalizations in (80)–(81), a syntactic mechanism is called for that cancels island violations in a syntactically limited context. Against these backgrounds, the next section evaluates some of the accounts of ellipsis proposed in the literatures.

4 Three Preceding Accounts

This section examines accounts of island repair proposed in the literature, which can be grouped into three categories. The question to be addressed here is whether any of these accounts is consistent with the observation made in the preceding sections that not all elliptical constructions can cancel island violations, more specifically, our generalizations in (80)–(81).

To anticipate our conclusion, we will see that only one of the accounts,

LF-copying account (Chung, Ladusaw, and McCloskey 1995), is consistent with our observations. We will therefore adopt the account and develop it further in the more recent framework.

*4.1 *-Marking and PF-Deletion*
The current standard explanation of island repair is the one proposed by Chomsky (1972) and adopted in one way or another by various authors (Bošković 2001, Fox and Lasnik 2003). At the heart of the proposal are the assumptions listed below.

(82) *-marking: When a phrase moves out of an island, the island is marked with *, a PF-uninterpretable feature.

(83) Elliptical phrases are present throughout the derivation but delete at PF.

(84) *can delete along with the elliptical phrase when the entire island is elided (Bošković 2011, Chomsky 1972).

The assumption in (82) puts * on the *wh*-island in (85), since extraction of *what* crosses the wh-island, *how John could eat*. Since * is PF-uninterpretable, the derivation will crash at PF if the phrase marked with * remains undeleted until PF. However, deleting the entire TP_E in (85) can wipe out * from the PF-representation, and the representation converges at PF. This is how the *-marking account works.

(85) [$_{TPA}$ Agnes wonders how John could eat something disgusting], but it's not clear what <$_{TPE}$ Agnes wonders *[how John could eat t$_i$]>

From the viewpoint of our generalizations, an obvious problem with this account is that it erroneously predicts that island repair takes place in every syntactic context. Nonetheless, we have seen a variety of syntactic contexts where island repair fails to take place. For instance, it fails to account for the fact that adjunct sluicing cannot repair island violations, since when the *-marked island disappears at PF, the PF representation would converge, an incorrect prediction.

(86) *[$_A$ Agnes wonders how John could eat], but it's not clear what <$_E$ Agnes wonders *[how John could eat t$_i$]>

Thus, the *-marking account fails to account for cases of ellipsis that do not repair islands, and encounters an empirical difficulty here. The same criticism applies when Japanese sentences are taken into consideration. For example, eliding the *-marked complex NP along with the rest of the clause in the second sentence in *also*-RD constructions should eliminate ungrammaticality in (87), but this expectation is not fulfilled.

(87) *Taroo-ga   [Yamada-sensei-ga   Hanako-o   sikatta   toyuu
     Taroo-NOM   Yamada-teacher-NOM   Hanako-ACC   scolded   that
     uwasa-o]   kinisiteru-yo,   Yoshiko-mo   <Taroo-ga
     rumor-ACC   is worried about   Yoshiko-also   Taroo-NOM
     *[Yamada-sensei-ga   sikatta   toyuu   uwasa-o]   kinisiteru>.
     Yamada-teacher-NOM   scolded   that   rumor-ACC   is worried about
     'Taroo is worried about the rumor that Professor Yamada scolded Hanako, (he is also worried about the rumor that Professor Yamada also scolded Yoshiko.'

Thus, our observation that island repair takes place only in a proper subset of elliptical constructions constitutes an obstacle for the *-marking account of island repair.

4.2 Propositional Islands

Another explanation of island repair gives a completely different representation to those elliptical sentences that appear to violate island constraints (Barros, Elliott, and Thoms 2014, Merchant 2001). The basic idea is that island repair is only apparent, since there is no island violation to begin with. Generally, the claim is that a propositional phrase contained in the island serves as an antecedent. Following Merchant (2001), we can call such an account the propositional island account. For instance, the antecedent for the elliptical phrase TP_E in (88) is TP_A in square brackets.

(88) Agnes wonders how [$_{TPA}$ John could eat something disgusting], but it's not clear what <$_{TPE}$ John could eat t>.

Our observations in the preceding sections constitute an insurmountable problem for this line of analysis. Under the propositional island account, sprouting and so many other instances of ellipsis should be free from island violations. This is because if (88) is a possible representation, so should be (89), which assumes that TP_A contained in the island is the antecedent for the elliptical phrase, TP_E.

(89) *Agnes wonders how [$_{TPA}$ John could eat], but it's not clear what <$_{TPE}$ John could eat t>.

This account also encounters a problem in explaining Japanese data. We have seen that when the antecedent clause in RD constructions contain a distal demonstrative coreferential with the dislocated phrase, island violations are canceled, but sprouting RD constructions fail to repair island violations. That (90) is grammatical means, under the propositional island account, that the elided phrase is simply *Professor Yamada scolded (the student)*. Exactly the same proposition should be available for (91) as the antecedent for elliptical phrase, but this falsely predicts that (91) is grammatical.

(90) Taroo-ga [Yamada-sensei-ga ano-gakusei$_i$-o sikatta toyuu
Taroo-NOM Yamada-teacher-NOM the student-ACC scolded that
uwasa-o] kinisiteru-yo, Hanako-o$_i$ <Yamada-sensei-ga
rumor-ACC is worried about Hanako-ACC Yamada teacher-NOM
sikatta>.
scolded
'Taroo is worried about the rumor that Professor Yamada scolded the student, Hanako.'

(91) *Taroo-ga [Yamada-sensei-ga sikatta toyuu uwasa-o]
Taroo-NOM Yamada-teacher-NOM scolded that rumor-ACC
kinisiteru-yo, Hanako-o <Yamada-sensei-ga sikatta>.
is worried about Hanako-ACC Yamada teacher-NOM scolded
'Taroo is worried about the rumor that Professor Yamada scolded, Hanako.'

Thus, the propositional island account of island repair also runs into difficulty when we take into account our observation that not all ellipsis allows island repair.

4.3 LF-Copying

4.3.1 LF-Copying and Island Repair

The final account we examine here of island repair is the one proposed in Chung, Ladusaw, and McCloskey (1995). The basic idea is that elliptical phrases are empty throughout the derivation, but have their antecedent copied at LF. The indefinite phrase in the antecedent clause acts as a variable to be bound by the remnant *wh*-phrase, once the antecedent clause is copied to the ellipsis site. In (92), for example, the indefinite phrase in the antecedent, *something disgusting*, is turned into a variable to be bound by the remnant *wh*-phrase, *what*, when the antecedent TP$_A$ is copied to the TP$_E$ site.

(92) Agnes wonders how John could eat something disgusting, but it's not clear what.

(93)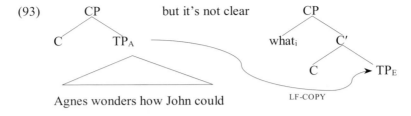

eat {something disgusting / t }ᵢ

Assuming that the subjacency condition is a derivational condition, the elliptical TP contains no violation of the condition, since the indefinite phrase interpreted as a variable simply gets bound by the *wh*-remnant, hence island repair.

4.3.2 Phase Recycling

One immediate consequence of the LF-copying account of island repair is that it predicts that whenever the antecedent lacks an indefinite phrase that serves as a variable to be bound by the remnant phrase, LF-copying cannot give rise to a licit representation. This predicts that, under the assumption that binding holds only of arguments, adjuncts sluicing are unable to get a proper interpretation through LF copying. Another prediction is that, in sprouting sentences, that lacks a correlate phrase in the antecedent cannot provide a variable to be bound by the remnant phrase. For example, simple copying of the antecedent TP in the sprouting sentence in (94) would result in the remnant phrase as a vacuous quantifier, and therefore is not permissible.

(94) [TPA He finished on time], but [with whose help]ᵢ <TPE he finished on time>?

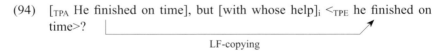

Note that this erroneously predicts that sprouting is generally impossible, even without an island violation, since sprouting in general results in vacuous quantification.

The problem pointed out above is by no means limited to sprouting in general. Contrastive *else* sluicing also suffers from the same difficulty, if the antecedent is simply copied to the ellipsis site, since the *wh*-remnant phrase has no variable to bind.

(95) [TPA HARRY came], but I don't know who else <TPE HARRY came>.

The same problem arises in the case of sprouting RD sentences and *also*-RD sentences in Japanese, shown below.

(96) [$_{TPA}$ Hanako-o   sikatta]-yo, Yamada-sensei-ga$_i$ <$_{TPE}$ Hanako-o
     Hanako-ACC scolded   Yamada teacher-NOM   Hanako-ACC
sikatta>.
scolded
'He scolded Hanako, Professor Yamada.'

(97) [$_{TPA}$ Yamada-sensei-ga   Hanako-o   sikatta]-yo, Sato-sensei-mo$_i$
     Yamada teacher-NOM Hanako-ACC scolded   Sato teacher-also
<$_{TPE}$ Yamada-sensei-ga   Hanako-o   sikatta>.
     Yamada teacher-NOM Hanako-ACC scolded
'Professor Yamada scolded Hanako, Professor Sato (also scolded Hanako).'

It is obvious that the proper representations we need for (94)–(97) are the ones given in (98)–(100) with the variable bound by the remnant *wh*-phrase.

(98) [$_{TPA}$ He finished on time], but [with whose help]$_i$ <$_{TPE}$ he finished on time t$_i$>?

(99) [$_{TPA}$ HARRY came], but I don't know who else <$_{TPE}$ t$_i$ came>.

(100) [$_{TPA}$ Hanako-o sikatta]-yo, Yamada-sensei-ga$_i$ <$_{TPE}$ t$_i$ Hanako-o sikatta>.
      [$_{TPA}$ Yamada-sensei-ga Hanako-o sikatta]-yo, Sato-sensei-mo$_i$ <$_{TPE}$ t$_i$ Hanako-o sikatta>.

It is clear that what we need here is a mechanism that adds a variable within the ellipsis site to be bound by the remnant *wh*-phrase, so that the remnant phrase has a variable to bind. We suggest that such a phrase is constructed through a process called phase recycling.

4.3.3 Phase Recycling

We would like to suggest that ellipsis in these constructions is established under identity with a recycled phase. Phase recycling uses Lexical Array (LA) that is a union of those of the antecedent and the remnant. In the case of (94), repeated as (101), the remnant *wh*-phrase itself has LF in (104), the union of (102) and (103).

(101) [$_{TPA}$ He finished on time], but [with whose help]$_i$ <$_{TPE}$ he finished on time>?

(102) {with, whose, help}

(103) {he, finished, on, time}

(104) {with, whose, help} U {he, finished, on, time}

Marge and move would result in the representation in (105), where <*with whose help*> in the angled brackets is the copy left behind by movement of the PP.

(105)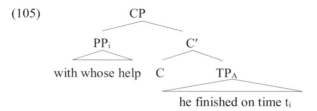

The TP$_A$ constructed through phase recycling has a proper form with a variable that can be bound by the remnant *wh*-phrase.

4.3.4 LF-Copying or PF-Deletion

The previous section advances the assumption that when the antecedent TP does not contain a variable to be bound by the remnant phrase, a proper antecedent is created based on the LA for the antecedent clause and the remnant phrase, a process we call phase recycling. The question we have to address is whether the recycled phrase is copied at LF to the ellipsis site (LF-copying), or the elliptical phrase is derivationally active that gets elided at PF under identity with the recycled phrase (PF-deletion). As far as we can see, the choice between in the two should be made on empirical grounds, but the two approaches seem to be empirically equivalent. We therefore suggest that the former approach, LF-copying, suffers from two theoretical difficulties, from which the PF-deletion approach is free.

One theoretical difficulty with adopting the LF-copying approach to phase recycling is that the recycled TP such as TP$_A$ in (105) contains all the features, including phonological features, that need to be spelt out to the PF component, since by assumption, the LA are recycled to form the phrase. Copying TP$_A$ with phonological features at LF to the ellipsis site results in a representation that cannot converge at LF and the derivation therefore crashes.

The second difficulty with the LF-copying approach has to do with the Inclusiveness condition of Chomsky (1995), which precludes introducing features to the derivation aside from those that is already specified in the lexical array (LA). The problem has to do with the fact that there are a number of elliptical constructions that obey island conditions, as we have observed extensively above. For example, (106) and (107) are sprouting sentences in English, which violate the *wh*-island condition and the subject condition, respectively.

(106) *Agnes wondered how John could eat, but it's not clear what <Agnes wondered *how John could eat t*>.

(106) *Agnes wondered how John could eat, but it's not clear what <Agnes wondered *how John could eat t*>.

(107) *That Tom would win is likely, but I am not sure which race <*that Tom would win t* is likely>.

The problem here is that to capture the island violation cases under the LF-copying approach, some versions of (82), repeated in (103), must be adopted.

(108) *-marking: When an island is crossed, islands are marked with *, a PF uninterpretable feature.

The recycled CP would look like (109) for the sentence in (106). The embedded CP is a *wh*-island, out of which the *wh*-phrase has been extracted, which therefore is *-marked.

(109) [$_{CP}$ what$_i$ [$_{TPA}$ Agnes wondered *[$_{CP}$ how John could eat t$_i$]]

Copying the recycled TP at LF results in a representation that is not interpretable at LF, assuming that * is not LF interpretable. This account, however, is not consistent with the inclusiveness condition, since it has a *-feature not specified in the LA and therefore should be abandoned if we are to maintain the inclusiveness condition.

The account based on PF-deletion is free from these difficulties.[2] Note

---

[2] We assume that ellipsis in general requires syntactic identity (Tanaka 2011c). This is based on the observation that the antecedent and the elliptical phrase must match in syntactic categories. A TP can be antecedent for sluicing (i), and so can be a clausal gerund (ii), but Ing-*of* gerunds fail to serve as antecedent for sluicing (iii).

that under the PF-deletion account, TP_A in (105) is constructed independently of the elliptical TP_E in (110), which itself is full-fledged throughout the derivation.

(110)   [$_{TPX}$ He finished on time], but [with whose help]$_i$ <$_{TPE}$ he finished on time>?

TP_E is then elided at PF against the recycled TP_A in (105), not against the TP_X in (110). TP_E itself has undergone full derivation prior to deletion, and contains no LF-uninterpretable features, since phonological features have been spelt out to PF.

Note also that there is no need to posit the *-marking mechanism in order to account for subjacency effects. (101), repeated in (111), would violate the *wh*-island condition within the ellipsis site. Assuming that subjacency is a derivational condition, (111) is automatically ruled out.

(111)   *Agnes wondered how John could eat, but it's not clear what$_i$ <Agnes wondered *how John could eat t$_i$*>.

Thus, the PF-deletion account of ellipsis works well for these cases. We have already seen that the only account consistent with our observation that island repair occurs only in a proper subset of elliptical constructions is LF-copying. The elliptical TP must contain either an indefinite, as in English sluicing constructions, or an NP coreferential with the dislocated phrase, as in Japanese RD constructions for island repair to take place. Given the fact that those elliptical constructions that fail to repair island violations call for PF-deletion means that a proper account of ellipsis requires both PF-deletion and LF-copying. As a matter of fact, the current minimalist program, which has two interface levels (articulatory-perceptual and conceptual-intentional interfaces) seems to allow both of these accounts of ellipsis, and precluding

(i)   I remember that we shot the scene, but I don't remember when.
(ii) I remember shooting the scene, but I don't remember when.
(iii) *I remember the shooting of the scene, but I don't remember when.

The conditions on ellipsis we adopt are the followings (Tanaka 2011:101);

(iv) Isomorphism condition on ellipsis XP_E can delete if and only if there is a contextually salient antecedent XP_A and XP_A and XP_E are β-variants.

(v)   Two expressions are β-variants if and only if β-marked expressions with some index in XP_A are consistently replaced with another β-marked index, and nothing else changes between the two sets.

one of them without a principled explanation amounts to a stipulation. Put another way, the proposal here serves as an argument against mono-stratal theories of grammar in general, since our proposal requires two different derivational points for ellipsis to take place.

4.3.5 VP-Ellipsis and Phase

The remaining question is why antecedent contained deletion (ACD) cannot repair locality violations. The relevant ACD example is repeated here.

(112) *John visited a city near every lake Op_i that Tom did <visited a city near t_i>.

The problem that (112) poses is that after QR, the antecedent VP looks like VP_A in (113).

(113) [every lake Op_i that Tom did <$_{VPE}$ visit a city near t_i>]$_i$ John [$_{VPA}$ visited a city near t_i]
         LF-copying

The VP_A in (113) has a variable, which can be bound by Op_i when the VP_A is copied to the VP_E site. LF-copying should therefore be available in (112), and we therefore erroneously predict that the ACD example in (112) is free from locality conditions, and that (112) should be grammatical.

I would like to suggest that VP-deletion cannot be interpreted through LF-copying because VP is not a phrase complement. Consider the skeletal clause structure in (114).

(114)

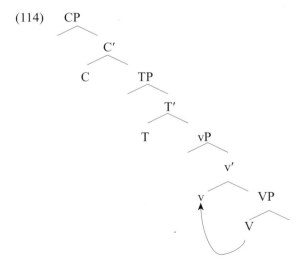

The two phase heads we find in (114) are C and v. Upon the completion of each phase, their complement, TP and VP, are transferred to the interface levels.

Since the verb in English raises overtly to v, what actually is elided in VP-deletion must be the higher verbal projection, vP, or else, the verb head would be stranded when VP-deletion applies.

(115) John visited a city. Bill did [$_{vP}$ visit$_i$ [~~$_{VP}$ t$_i$ a city~~]], too.

Note, however, that vP is not a phrase complement. Suppose that LF-copying is subject to the following intuitively reasonable condition.

(116) At the CI interface, only phase complements are visible, and no other phrases are available for interpretation, including LF-copying.

Given (116), vPs, not being a phase complement, cannot be copied. Hence, elliptical vPs cannot be interpreted through LF-copying. Instead, they must be active throughout the derivation, and the relative operator in (112), repeated below, must therefore move out of the PP headed by *near*, which gives rise to a violation of locality conditions.

(117) *John visited a city near every lake Op$_i$ that Tom did <visited a city near t$_i$>.

We thus predict that VP-deletion, including ACD, cannot cancel island violations.

5 Summary

In this article, we have seen that island repair fails to take place in a variety of elliptical constructions both in English and Japanese: island repair is limited to English sluicing and Japanese RD constructions with a correlate phrase in the antecedent coreferential with the dislocated constituent. Among various accounts of island repair offered in the literature, only the LF copying account is compatible with our observation. Elliptical constructions that fail to repair island violations, such as sprouting, *wh-else* sluicing, and adjunct sluicing cannot have the antecedent TP copied at LF, because binding is impossible. Similarly, RD constructions in Japanese must have a correlate phrase coreferential with the dislocated phrase in order for binding to be possible after copying, a prerequisite for island repair. When this fails, island violations cannot be canceled, and phase must be recycled to create an antecedent with a proper variable, which can cause violations of island conditions. Antecedent contained deletion (ACD) poses an interesting case, since the construction can provide a variable to be bound by the relative operator. Nevertheless, island repair fails to take place in ACD. The reason for that, we have seen, is that LF-copying of vPs is generally impossible, since only transferred phrases, that is, phase complements (TP or VP), can be copied at LF.

References

Barros, Matthew, Patrick Elliott, and Gary Thoms. 2014. There is no island repair. Ms., Rutgers University, University College of London, and the University of Edinburgh.
Bošković, Željko. 2011. Rescue by PF deletion, traces as (non)interveners, and the that-trace effect. *Linguistic Inquiry* 42:1–44.
Chomsky, Noam. 1972. Some empirical issues in the theory of transformational grammar. In *Goals of linguistic theory*, ed. by Paul Stanley Peters, 260–285. Englewood Cliffs, N.J.: Prentice-Hall.
Chomsky, Noam. 1981. *Lectures on government and binding*. Dordrecht: Foris.
Chomsky, Noam. 1995. *The minimalist program*. Cambridge, MA: MIT Press.
Chomsky, Noam. 2008. On phases. In *Foudational issues in linguistic theory: Essays in Honor of Jean-Roger Vergnaud*, ed. by Robert Freidin, Carlos P Otero, and Maria Luisa Zubizarreta, 133–166. Cambridge, MA: MIT Press.
Chung, Sandra, William A. Ladusaw, and James McCloskey. 1995. Sluicing and logical form. *Natural Language Semantics* 3:239–282.
Fox, Danny, and Howard Lasnik. 2003. Successive-cyclic movement and island repair: The difference between sluicing and VP-ellipsis. *Linguistic Inquiry* 34:143–154.
Harada, Shin-Ichi. 1977. Nihongo-ni 'henkei'-wa hituyoo-da [Transformation is neccesarry in Japanese]. *Gengo* 6:11–12.
Huang, Cheng-Teh James. 1982. Logical relations in Chinese and the theory of grammar. Doctoral dissertation, MIT, Cambridge, MA.
Kennedy, Christopher. 1997. Antecedent-contained deletion and the syntax of quantification. *Linguistic Inquiry* 28:662–668.
May, Robert. 1985. *Logical form: Its structure and derivation*. Cambridge, MA: MIT Press.
Merchant, Jason. 2001. *The syntax of silence: Sluicing, islands, and the theory of ellipsis*. Oxford: Oxford University Press.
Ross, John Robert. 1967. Constraints on variables in syntax. Doctoral dissertaion, MIT, Cambirdge, MA.
Ross, John Robert. 1969. Guess who? In *Proceedings of the fifth regional meeting of the Chicago Linguistic Society*, ed. by Robert I. Binnick, 252–286. Chicago: Department of Linguistics, University of Chicago.
Saito, Mamoru. 1985. Some asymmetries in Japanese and their theoretical implica-

tions. Doctoral dissertaion, MIT, Cambridge, MA.

Sauerland, Uli. 1997. Guess how. In *Proceedings of the fourth Conference of the Student Organization of Linguistics in Europe (CONSOLE)*, ed. by João Costa, Rob Goedemans, and Ruben van de Vijver, 297–309. Leiden: Student Organization of Linguistics in Europe.

Tanaka, Hidekazu. 1996. Right-dislocation in Japanese. *McGill Working Papers in Linguistics* 11:105–124.

Tanaka, Hidekazu. 2001. Right-dislocation as scrambling. *Journal of Linguistics* 37:551–579.

Tanaka, Hidekazu. 2011a. Antecedent contained deletion in the domain of a raised object. *The Linguistic Review* 31:401–434.

Tanaka, Hidekazu. 2011b. Voice mismatch and syntactic identity. *Linguistic Inquiry* 42:470–507.

Tanaka, Hidekazu. 2011c. Syntactic identity and ellipsis. *The Linguistic Review* 28:79–110.

Verbal Affix Deletion in Indonesian Quotative Inversion

Kazuhide Chonan

> One of the interesting phenomena in Indonesian syntax is verbal affix deletion. Transitive and unergative verbal roots are prefixed with *meN-* and *ber-*, respectively. The affixes are deleted in seemingly unrelated constructions: zero-passive, relative clause, imperative, and quotative inversion. Focusing on the last construction, this paper compares the syntactic and information structures of quotative inversion in English and Indonesian, and claims that Quote, the verb, and the subject are positioned higher in Indonesian than in English, based mainly on the distribution of floated quantifiers and the distinction of old/new information within the construction. Setting aside the affix deletion in zero-passive, the paper makes the generalization that a verbal root cannot bear more than one V-related feature in Indonesian, unlike the finite copular and aspectual verbs in English, which are assumed to move from V to C via T in matrix questions. The contrast in the two languages is arguably minimum in the sense that the same constraint is operative in English embedded clauses as well.
>
> *Keywords:* Quotative Inversion, information structure, verbal affixes, roots

1 Deletion of the Verbal Affixes *meN-* and *ber-*

Almost all transitive verbs in Indonesian have the prefix *meN-*, while unergative verbs have *ber-*.

(1) a. John **mem-**baca buku itu.
      John MEN-read book the
      'John reads the book.'
   b. John **be-r**enang.[1]
      John BER-swim
      'John swims.'

---

[1] The root of the verb *berenang* is not *enang* but *renang*. The final consonant of the prefix is fused with the following.

Following Hale and Keyser (1993, 2002), I assume that transitive and unergative verbs are composed of roots and light verbs. In Indonesian, the latter are morphologically realized as *meN-* and *ber-*, respectively, while they are phonologically null in English.

What is interesting about the prefixes in Indonesian is that they are deleted in a number of seemingly unrelated constructions. First, *meN-* is deleted in so-called zero-passive (Passive type two[2]) as in (2), within relative clause as in (3), and in imperative as in (4).

(2) Buku itu John φ-baca.
    book the John read
    'The book is read by John.'

(3) Saya meminjam buku [yang John φ-baca].
    I borrow book C John read
    'I borrowed the book which John read.'

(4) φ-Baca buku itu!
    read book the
    'Read the book!'

It is standardly assumed that A-movement is involved in (2), A'-movement in (3), and neither in (4). Why does *meN-* get deleted in these three constructions?

As for the unergative prefix *ber-*, it appears with verbs of saying as in (5a). (5a) has the corresponding inverted structure (5b), where *ber-* is obligatorily deleted.

(5) a. John ber-kata, "Terima kasih."
      John BER-say Thank you
   b. "Terima kasih," kata John.
      "Thank you" φ-say John

A question arises if the deletion in (5b) falls under the deletion phenomena exemplified in (2)–(4). Note that (5b) looks quite similar to Quotative Inversion in English like (6b).

(6) a. John said, "Thank you."

---

[2] The construction exemplified by (2) is called variously in the literature. Chung (1972) calls it "object preposing," while Sneddon (2010), "passive type two." We will call it here as "zero-passive," since verbs have no affixes in this construction.

b. "Thank you," said John.

Both (5b) and (6b) have non-canonical word orders: Q(uotative)-V(erb)-S(ubject), but I will argue that they have distinct syntactic and information structures.

In this paper, I will first elucidate the properties of English and Indonesian Quotative Inversion, and argue that their differences come from different syntactic structures in the two languages: in English, Quote (Q) is in [Spec, TP], while in Indonesian, it is in [Spec, CP]. Then I will argue that verbal affix deletion in Indonesian Quotative Inversion is closely connected with the fundamental architecture of its clausal structure, and the proposal has some implications for the Phase theory.

2 Quotative Inversion in the Previous Studies

2.1 Comparison between Indonesian and English Quotative Inversion
This section compares Indonesian and English Quotative Inversion closely, pointing out similarities and differences between them.

In both languages, Inversion is optional. In English, when Quote is located sentence-initial, both Q-V-S order in (7a) and Q-S-V order in (7b) are allowed. Similarly, in Indonesian, both Q-V-S order in (8a) and Q-S-V order in (8b) are allowed. Note that only when the order is Q-V-S as in (8a), the verbal affix *ber-* is obligatorily deleted.

   (7) English
      a. "Thank you," said John.
      b. "Thank you," John said.

   (8) Indonesian
      a. "Terima kasih," kata   John.
         Thank you   φ-say   John
      b. "Terima kasih," John   ber-kata.
         Thank you   John   BER-say

When the sentence contains auxiliaries or negatives, inversion is impossible as shown in (9–12) (Collins 1997:34).

   (9) English, with auxiliaries
      a. *"Thank you," must say John.
      b. *"Thank you," say must John.
      c. *"Thank you," must John say.

(10) English, with negatives
    a. *"Thank you," not said John.
    b. *"Thank you," didn't say John.
    c. *"Thank you," said not John.
    d. *"Thank you," say didn't John.
    e. *"Thank you," didn't John say.

(11) Indonesian, with auxiliaries
    a. *"Terima kasih," harus kata John.
        Thank you must say John
    b. *"Terima kasih," kata harus John.
        Thank you say must John
    c. *"Terima kasih," harus John kata.
        Thank you must John say

(12) Indonesian, with negatives
    a. *"Terima kasih," tidak kata John.
        Thank you not say John
    b. *"Terima kasih," kata tidak John.
        Thank you say not John
    c. *"Terima kasih," tidak John kata.
        Thank you not John say

However, Indonesian Quotative Inversion exhibits different characteristics from those in English. First, as pointed out above, the verbal suffix *ber*- is deleted obligatorily in Indonesian. Its function has not been clarified yet, but *ber*- can be considered to be a kind of verbalizer or light verb (Chonan 2010). English does not have a comparable verbal suffix; hence, no deletion of a verbal suffix in English.

Second, the two constructions are used in different styles. English Quotative Inversion is used in written style, while Indonesian inversion is colloquial.

Third, English and Indonesian Quotative Inversion impose distinct restrictions on the type of subject. In English, a common noun is possible but a pronoun is avoided, as in (13) (Collins 1997:33). On the contrary, in Indonesian, pronominal subjects are preferred, as in (14b).

(13) English
    a. "Thank you," said the man.
    b. "Thank you," said ?he/*him.

(14) Indonesian
    a. "Terima kasih," kata orang itu.
        Thank you say man the
    b. "Terima kasih," kata dia / kata-nya.
        Thank you say he / say-he

Furthermore, in English Quotative Inversion, the subject can be quite complex as in (15a). However, in Indonesian, the complex subject reduces the acceptability of the construction as in (15b).[3]

(15) a. "Thank you," said the man who came from Japan.
    b. ?"Terima kasih," kata orang yang datang dari Jepang.
       Thank you say man who come from Japan.

These facts indicate that the subject in Indonesian Quotative Inversion cannot express important or new information.

Fourth, Quantifier Floating is impossible in English Quotative Inversion, while in Indonesian, it is possible, which will be discussed shortly.

In sum, Indonesian Quotative Inversion appears to be similar to the English construction, except for the verbal affix deletion phenomenon. However, Indonesian Quotative Inversion has several unique characteristics. We will attempt to deduce these properties from the basic clausal structure, which is different from English. In the following sections, we will examine syntactic structures of English and Indonesian Quotative Inversion.

2.2 Previous Study on English Quotative Inversion: Collins (1997)

Among a few studies on English Quotative Inversion, I focus on Collins (1997). Collins and Branigan (1997) make a slightly different claim, but I do not go into its detail since the differences are essentially notational. In this section, following Collins (1997), I will confirm the syntactic structure of English Quotative Inversion.

Collins (1997) discusses where the subject, the verb, and Quote are located in English Quotative Inversion. Let us see them in order.

---

[3] Most native speakers judge (15b) as unnatural, while others as grammatical. Diversity of judgement may come from the status of *yang* phrases. *Yang* phrases in Indonesian are considered to be relative clauses, but the difference between restrictive and nonrestrictive use is not clear. The former may judge *yang* phrases as restrictive relatives, while the latter as nonrestrictive. Indonesian imposes a constraint on information structure as will be discussed below: The subject must express old information. Nonrestrictive relatives can add new information to the subject.

First, on the position of the subject, Collins (1997) argues that the subject does not move to the right based on a pair of examples in (16).

(16) a. "Where to?" asked the driver of the passenger.
b. *"Where to?" asked of the passenger the driver.
(Collins 1997:32)

If the subject moves from the normal position (e.g., [Spec, TP]) to the right periphery of the sentence, the resultant word order must be (16b). However, (16b) is ungrammatical. This fact suggests that the subject does not undergo rightward movement.

Next, let us see how Quotative Inversion interacts with Quantifier Floating. Quantifier Floating in English has been considered to help clarify the surface subject position under the VP-internal subject hypothesis; a quantifier can be stranded within VP when the subject moves into [Spec, TP] (Koopman and Sportiche 1991, Haegeman 2005). (17a) has the canonical word order, and the quantifier *all* can be floated, as shown in (17b). (17c) has the inverted word order, and the quantifier cannot be stranded, as in (17d).

(17) a. "We must do this again," [$_{NP}$ all the guests] declared to Tony.
b. "We must do this again," [$_{NP}$ the guests] [all] declared to Tony.
c. "We must do this again," declared [$_{NP}$ all the guests] to Tony.
d. *"We must do this again," declared [$_{NP}$ the guests] [all] to Tony.
(Collins 1997:33)

The ungrammaticality of (17d) suggests that the subject in English Quotative Inversion stays within VP.

Next, let us consider the position of the verb. As has been shown in Section 1, Quotative Inversion is incompatible with negation, as repeated in (18). Collins (1997) argues that this fact is due to V-raising. Collins assumes that a main verb is raised to T in this construction, which generally cannot occur in English. When a negative head (Neg) is present between T and the verb, Neg prohibits movement of the verb to T.

(18) a. *"Let's eat," not said John just once.
b. *"Let's eat," said not John just once.
c. *"Let's eat," didn't John say just once.
(Collins 1997:33)

The ungrammaticality of (18a–c) suggests that the main verb should be under T in English Quotative Inversion.

Concerning the position of Quote, it is clearly to the left of the verb, which is in T. Then, the most plausible position is [Spec, TP].[4]

Finally, Collins (1997) concludes that Quotative Inversion in English has syntactic structure (19).

(19) Structure of English Quotative Inversion
(Collins 1997:40, modified by the author)[5]

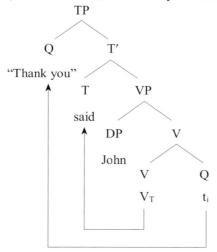

According to this analysis, Quote is located in [Spec TP], which is the normal subject position in English, the verb is raised to T, and the subject stays in [Spec VP]. This structure has been shown to explain several syntactic facts such as non-cooccurrence with negatives.

---

[4] In this construction, the parenthetical construction below is also possible.

(i) "John," said Mary, "wants to go to the store."
(Collins 1997:39)

Thus, Collins argues that an operator rather than Quote is in [Spec, TP]. In order to make the discussion simpler, I consider Quote itself is in [Spec, TP]. The discussion so far by Collins (1997) does not exclude the possibility that Quote moves further to the left through [Spec, TP], such as [Spec, CP]. Collins himself admit that there is no evidence for the movement of the Quote to the left such as [Spec, CP].

[5] This structure differs from the one proposed in Collins (1992:40) in two respects. First, Collins argues that it is an operator that is in [Spec, TP]. Second, Collins postulates Tr(ansitive) phrase between TP and VP, and the subject is in [Spec, TrP] rather than [Spec VP]. These two points are not crucial to the argument here.

2.3 Previous Study on Indonesian: Sneddon (2010)

Although Indonesian Quotative Inversion has not elicited much attention in syntactic research, Sneddon (2010) makes a notable claim on this construction. Sneddon (2010) argues that what appears to be a verb in this construction is actually a noun. For example, the word *kata* in (20) is the root of the verb *berkata* 'say'.

(20) Sneddon's Analysis
    "Terima kasih," kata John.
    Thank you   word John
                   N   N (Possessor)

Actually, the word *kata* can be used as a noun, which has the meaning 'word'. According to Sneddon, *kata* and *John* in (20) are both nouns. So, this construction is not Q-V-S, but has Q-N-N structure. The sentence is claimed to have the meaning: "Thank you" is John's word.

Sneddon's analysis is interesting in that it reflects native speakers' intuition that this construction must somehow be different from English Quotative Inversion. His analysis, however, has many shortcomings. First, let us consider the meaning of this construction. According to his analysis, (21b) means that "Thank you" is John's word. However, the non-inverted construction in (21a) has the interpretation '"Thank you," John said' because the word *berkata* with the verbal affix *ber-* must unambiguously be a verb.

(21) a. "Terima kasih," John ber-kata.
        Thank you   John BER-say
    b. "Terima kasih," kata John.
        Thank you   word John

In fact, (21a,b) are felt to mean essentially the same, which suggests that *kata* in (21b) is also verbal.

Second, according to this analysis, (21b) does not involve inversion, but a kind of copular sentence. However, there is much evidence that (21b) is not a copular sentence. In Indonesian, copular sentences have unique characteristics, different from sentences with non-copular verbs. For example, in copular sentences, copular words such as *adalah* can be inserted optionally as in (22a), and the word *bukan* is used in negative sentences, while *tidak* is used in normal sentences, as in (22b).

(22) a. John adalah murid.
        John COPULA student

b. John <u>bukan</u> murid.
   John not   student

Quotative Inversion does not allow these words, as in (23).

(23) a. *"Terima kasih," <u>adalah</u> sahut John.
        Thank you   COPULA answer John
   b. *"Terima kasih," <u>bukan</u> sahut John.
        Thank you   not   answer John

Third, it is true that the verbal root *kata* in (21b) has the usage as an independent noun but not all verbal roots can be used as nouns. The word *sahut* 'answer' in (23) is one of them; it cannot be used as a noun. Without *adalah/bukan*, (23a,b) are acceptable, but they cannot be regarded as copular constructions.

The foregoing discussions have revealed that the verb in Quotative Inversion cannot be analyzed as a noun. Moreover, there is further evidence on the status of the sentence-final noun *John*. According to Sneddon (2010), the noun *John* in Quotative Inversion is not a subject, but a possessor. However, *John* has typical properties of subject. Sneddon himself argues that the subject in Indonesian has some characteristics. In Indonesian, pronouns usually do not change their forms according to their grammatical functions, but the third person singular pronoun *ia* is used only as subject, as in (24a); it cannot be used in the position of possessor, as in (24b).

(24) a. Ia akan menolong kami.
      he will help   us
      'He will help us.'
   b. Ini buku *ia.
      it book his
      'It is his book.'
      (Sneddon 2010:169)

In Quotative Inversion, the pronoun *ia* can be used as in (25). Thus, the sentence-final noun in this construction must be the subject, rather than the possessor.

(25) "Terima kasih," kata ia.
     Thank you   say he

Enough evidence has been shown to disconfirm Sneddon's (2010) analysis. It can be concluded that Quotative Inversion in Indonesian is not a copular construction. The next section will propose a more plausible analysis of Indonesian Quotative Inversion.

3 Structure of Quotative Inversion

3.1 Quotative Inversion and Information Structure

Before discussing the syntactic structure, let us reconfirm some important differences between English and Indonesian Quotative Inversion. One of them is about the status of subject. In English, a pronominal subject is disallowed, as in (26b), while in Indonesian, it is allowed and in fact, preferred, as in (27b). Moreover, in English, the subject can be longer, as in (26c), while in Indonesian, the longer, heavier subject reduces acceptability, as in (27c).

(26) English
    a. "Thank you," said the man.
    b. "Thank you," said ?he/*him.
    c. "Thank you," said the man who came from Japan.

(27) Indonesian
    a. "Terima kasih," kata orang itu.
        Thank you say man the
    b. "Terima kasih," kata dia / kata-nya.
        Thank you say he / say-he
    c. ?"Terima kasih," kata orang yang datang dari Jepang.
        Thank you say man who come from Japan

These facts suggest that Quotative Inversion in the two languages have different information structures. In English, since a pronominal subject is not allowed, the whole sentence including the subject presents new information, as described in (28a). On the other hand, in Indonesian, since a pronominal subject is preferred and a heavy subject is not allowed, only the Quote expresses new information, and the subject, old.

(28) a. English: <u>"Thank you,"</u> <u>said John</u>.
                            new
    b. Indonesian: <u>"Terima kasih,"</u> kata <u>John</u>.
                              new   old

The contrastive information structures are the basis of deciding the syntactic structures of Quotative Inversion in the two languages.

3.2 Informational Constraint on Subject in Indonesian

In Indonesian, it has been pointed out that there is some constraint on the informational status of subject. In *wh*-questions, the object can freely be a *wh*-phrase, as in (29a), while the subject cannot, as in (29b).

(29) a. John mem-beli apa?
        John MEN-buy   what
        'What did John buy?'
    b. *Siapa mem-beli buku?
        who   MEN-buy   book
    c. Siapa yang mem-beli buku?
        who   C   MEN-buy   book
        'Who is the one who bought the book?'

When the subject is a *wh*-word, it is necessary to use the complementizer *yang*, and make the whole structure into a cleft, as in (29c).

To explain why (29b) is not allowed, Cole, Hermon, and Tjung (2005) propose the constraint in (30).

(30) Informational Constraint on Subject
      The new information must occur in the predicate and the subject must be the old information.
      (Cole, Hermon, and Tjung 2005:562)[6]

Paraphrasing (30) in terms of a more recent framework, 'the subject' in (30) is the surface subject, occupying [Spec, TP], while a VP-internal subject is part of the predicate. *Wh*-words correspond to new information, but the subject in [Spec, TP] must be old information. Thus, subject *wh*-questions are not allowed. (29c) is acceptable presumably because the phrase headed by *yang* is the logical subject and the *wh*-subject, the predicate.

3.3 Syntactic Structure of Indonesian Quotative Inversion

As illustrated in (28a), in Indonesian Quotative Inversion, Quote is new information, and the subject is old. It follows from the informational constraint on subject (30) that Quote (new information) must be located in the position other than the subject, that is, [Spec, CP], while the subject (old information) must be in [Spec, TP]. A heavy subject is not allowed in Quotative Inversion for the same reason as that for the unacceptability of subject *wh*-questions

---

[6] Cole, Hermon, and Tjung (2005) call this constraint "the Parallelism Hypothesis."

discussed in Section 3.2.

On the other hand, there is no evidence that English subjects must express old information (Matos 2013:126).[7] Thus, Quote can be located in subject position. This reasoning is consistent with the conclusion of Collins (1997): Quote is in [Spec, TP]. In this way, Indonesian and English Quotative Inversion can be assumed to have different information/syntactic structures.

Another piece of evidence on this analysis comes from Quantifier Floating. As pointed out in Section 2.1, Quantifier Floating is not allowed in English Quotative Inversion, as in (31b).

(31) a. "We must do this again," declared [NP all the guests] to Tony.
b. *"We must do this again," declared [NP the guests] [all] to Tony.
(Collins 1997:33)

On the other hand, Indonesian Quotative Inversion can cooccur with Quantifier Floating, as in (32b).[8]

(32) a. "Terima kasih," kata [NP tiga orang pegawai].
      Thank you say three person officer
b. "Terima kasih," kata [NP pegawai] [tiga orang].
      Thank you say officer three person

These facts also suggest that the subject in Indonesian Quotative Inversion is in [Spec, TP]; it expresses old information, obeying the informational constraint in (30).

In conclusion, English and Indonesian Quotative Inversion can be analyzed as having the structures given in (33a,b), respectively.

(33) a. [TP "Thank you," said [VP John ...]]
b. [CP "Terima kasih," kata [TP John [VP ...]]]

Quote is in [Spec, TP] in English but in [Spec, CP] in Indonesian. The subject stays in VP in English and is raised into [Spec, TP] in Indonesian.

---

[7] According to Matos (2013:126), in English, the subject presenting informational focus typically occurs in preverbal position.

[8] In Indonesian, universal quantifiers such as *all* cannot float. Thus, numerical expressions such as *three men* are used in Indonesian examples.

3.4 Notes on Locative Inversion

This section will briefly discuss another type of inversion, Locative Inversion. According to Collins (1997), English Locative Inversion is similar to Quotative Inversion: the locative phrase in (34b) is located in [Spec, TP], as Quote in (34a) (Collins 1997:29).

(34) a. "Thank you," said John.
b. In the village lived a king.

In Indonesian, however, Locative Inversion seems to be different from Quotative Inversion. In Quotative Inversion, the sentence-initial Quote expresses new information, while in Locative Inversion, the sentence initial locative phrase is old information, and the sentence-final subject, new, as described in (35) (Huddleston and Pullum 2005:258).

(35) a. "Terima kasih," kata John.
Thank you say John
New Old
b. Di kampung itu tinggal seorang raja.
in village the live one king
Old New
'In the village lived a king.'

Thus, it is assumed that Indonesian Quotative Inversion and Locative Inversion have different structures: Quote is located in [Spec, CP], while Locative, [Spec, TP], as in (36).

(36) a. Quotative Inversion
[$_{CP}$ "Terima kasih," kata [$_{TP}$ John [$_{VP}$]]]
b. Locative Inversion
[$_{TP}$ Di kampung itu tinggal [$_{VP}$ seorang raja]]

4 Ban on Multiple Verbal Features

This section will examine Quotative Inversion and other constructions in Indonesian which undergo verbal affix deletion.

Let us first consider the deletion of the verbal affix in Imperative. In affirmative imperative, the affix is deleted obligatorily, as in (37).

(37) a. φ-Baca buku itu!
read book the

b. *Mem-baca buku itu!
   MEN-read book the
   'Read the book!'

However, in negative imperative (38), the deletion is optional.

(38) a. Jangan φ-baca buku itu!
        not read book the
     b. Jangan mem-baca buku itu!
        not MEN-read book the
        'Don't read the book!'

The contrast must be accounted for.

Note that negative imperatives show distinct properties not only in Indonesian but also in many other languages (Bošković 2008). For example, in English imperatives, the verb *be* is negated by *don't*, rather than *not* as shown in (39a,b), while *be* can and must move over *not* in a declarative as shown in (39c,d).

(39) a. Don't be noisy!
     b. *Be not noisy!
     c. John is not noisy.
     d. *John does not be noisy.

Be does not move into T in imperative presumably because T does not exist or lacks a feature to attract a verb. If that is the case, the impossible order in imperative (39b) parallels that with finite main verbs as exemplified in (40).

(40) a. John laughed.
     b. *John not laughed.
     c. John did not laugh.

If affix hopping or PF merger of T with a verb requires linear adjacency as Bošković (2008) argues, it is blocked by *not* in (40b), and *do*-support, which is a last resort operation, applies as in (40c). Bošković assumes some functional category F above TP in imperatives to account for the distribution of clitics in Bulgarian and Macedonian. Adopting this idea, I claim that in affirmative imperatives, PF merger of F with *be* applies properly with no overt materials between them as described in (41a), while it is blocked in negative imperatives by intervening *not* in (41b).

(41) a. [F [TP T [VP be quiet]]]

b. [F [TP T not [VP be noisy]]]

Then, *do* is inserted to support F in (41b).

Going back to the Indonesian data, the head F assumed in imperatives is a bound morpheme and needs to be affixed onto some appropriate element.

(42) a. *[F [TP [vP meN- [VP baca buku]]]]
b. [F [TP [vP φ- [VP baca buku]]]]
c. [F [TP Jangan [vP φ-baca/ meN-baca buku]]]

If F is affixed onto the verb prefixed with *meN-* in (42a), the verbal root hosts two affixes, while it hosts just F in (42b). It can be said that each verbal root in Indonesian can host at most one verbal affix.[9] (42c) is acceptable probably because F is affixed onto the special negative word *jangan* just as F is affixed onto *do* in (41b).

In Quotative Inversion, the verb has been analyzed as moving to C. If C contains some abstract affix or feature that induces Quotative Inversion, it needs to be associated with the raised verb.

(43) [CP "Terima kasih" [C φ-kata/*ber-kata$_i$] [TP John [vP t$_i$]]]

The obligatory absence of *ber-* in this construction can be attributed to the requirement that each verbal root can host no more than one verbal feature or affix.

The absence of *meN-* in relative clauses in (3), repeated as (44), can be explained analogously.

(44) Saya meminjam buku [yang John φ-baca].
I borrow book C John read
'I borrowed the book which John read.'

I assume that an abstract operator (i.e., *op*) moves from object position into the specifier of CP headed by *yang* via [Spec, *v*P] as described in (45).

---

[9] In addition to prefixes such as *ber-* and *meN-*, there are some suffixes like *-kan*, and *-i* in Indonesian. It is possible for verbal roots to have both a prefix and a suffix. They can be considered to be high and low applicative heads, respectively (Chonan 2010). I propose the generalization in (46), which says that a verbal root cannot bear more than one V-related feature. If features of the Indonesian suffixes are not V-related in the sense here, (46) is not violated.

(45) [TP Saya T meminjam [NP buku [CP op_i [TP John [vP t_i [v φ-baca_j [VP t_j t_i]]]]]]]

If *op* can stop at [Spec, *v*P] only if the light verb head has some feature to induce that movement, the restriction on the verbal affix in a relative clause can be attributed to the restriction that is operative in imperative and Quotative Inversion. The discussion so far leads to the following generalization:

(46) A verbal root cannot bear more than one V-related feature in Indonesian.

V-related features in (46) include transitive and unergative markers, which are morphologically realized as *meN-* and *ber-*, respectively, the putative feature to induce the movement of *op* in (45), F in imperatives, and some feature under C to induce Quotative Inversion. The affixed verb is disallowed in (44) since the verbal root bears the affix as well as the feature to induce the movement of *op*, violating (46).

Does (46) hold in English? The answer seems to be negative, given the acceptability of (47a) analyzed as (47b).

(47) a. What are you going to read?
 b. [CP what [C be-T_Q]_j [TP you [T t_j] [VP t_j going to read t_i]]]

Be and auxiliary *have* can pick up T as well as Q, forming higher projections. As is well-known, however, they do not move up to C in embedded questions.

(48) a. I wonder what you are going to read.
 b. *I wonder what are you going to read.

Moreover, imperatives and Quotative Inversion are allowed in main clauses. I speculate that something like (46) operates in English as well and it is somehow relaxed in the root context.

Note that Quotative Inversion and Locative Inversion are allowed only in main clauses in English as shown in (49).

(49) a. *I was surprised when "Thank you," said John.
 b. *I hear that in the village lived a king.

In Indonesian, however, Quotative Inversion is impossible in subordinate clauses, but Locative Inversion is possible as in (50).

(50) a. *Saya terkejut ketika "Terima kasih," kata John.
       I surprised when thank you say John
    b. Saya dengar bahwa di kampung itu tinggal seorang raja.
       I hear that in village the live a king

This is due to the different syntactic structures of the constructions in the two languages. In English, both Quote in Quotative Inversion and the locative phrase in Locative Inversion are in [Spec, TP], while in Indonesian, Quote is in [Spec, CP], but the locative phrase is in [Spec TP], as discussed in the section 3.4.[10] (50a) is impossible because the complementizer *ketika* may not cooccur with the feature under C to induce Quotative Inversion. (50b) is possible because the locative phrase is in the specifier of TP selected by the complementizer *bahwa*.

5 Conclusion

This paper has worked on one of the interesting phenomena in Indonesian syntax: verbal affix deletion. Transitive and unergative verbal roots are canonically prefixed with *meN-* and *ber-*, respectively, and the affixes are obligatorily deleted in apparently unrelated constructions: Quotative Inversion, imperatives, and relative clauses. Deletion of affixes in these constructions has been argued to obey the constraint that a verbal root in Indonesian cannot bear more than one V-related feature to build up CP and other projections above TP via its iterative internal mergers. This constraint is presumably due to the total absence of agreement in Indonesian: No overt presence of tense-like elements, no overt subject-verb agreement, no subject-auxiliary inversion to form a question, no obligatory overt *wh*-movement, and even no distinction between copular and genitive constructions, as illustrated in (51).

(51) a. Kakak guru.
       brother teacher
       'The brother is a teacher.'
    b. kakak guru
       brother teacher
       'the teacher's brother'

---

[10] It is impossible to examine whether verbal affix deletion occurs in Locative Inversion, because verbs used in Locative Inversion are typically unaccusative, and in general unaccusative verbs in Indonesian do not have affixes.

Transitive and unergative verbs in their canonical positon are prefixed with *meN-* and *ber-*, respectively. To show that they are not in their canonical position, it is impossible to inflect them; instead, their prefixes are deleted to show that they are not in their canonical position.

The finite copular and aspectual verbs in English, on the other hand, can move up to C in matrix questions, which suggests that they can bear two V-related features: tense and Q. Still, they are like Indonesian verbs in that they do not undergo T-to-C movement in the embedded context and cannot bear an abstract feature to type imperatives. Clearly, the presence of Q in an embedded question is due to selection of a specific C by a higher predicate; Q and tense appear separately in the embedded context. The matrix T, on the other hand, can be analyzed as bundling Q as well as tense (see Grimshaw 1997 and Broekhuis 2013, Dikken 2006, Gallego and Uriagereka 2006). If T can bundle a feature to induce Quotative and Locative Inversion only in the matrix clause, these constructions are blocked in the embedded clause.

References

Bošković, Željko. 2008. When are negative imperatives banned? Ms., University of Connecticut, Storrs.

Broekhuis, Hans. 2013. Feature inheritance versus extended projections. Ms. Meertens Institute, Amsterdam.

Chonan, Kazuhide. 2010. *A study of causatives and applicatives in English, Indonesian, and other languages*. Doctoral dissertation, Dokkyo University, Saitama.

Chonan, Kazuhide. 2014. Indonesiago no inyoukutouchikoubun (Quotative Inversion in Indonesian). *Indonesia Gengo to Bunka* (Journal of Indonesian Studies Association in Japan) 20:94–112.

Chung, Sandra. 1972. On the subjects of two passives in Indonesian. In *Subject and topics*, ed. by Charles N. Li, 57–99. New York: Academic Press.

Cole, Peter, Gabriella Hermon, and Yassir Tjung. 2005. How irregular in WH in situ in Indonesian? *Studies in Language* 29:553–581.

Collins, Chris. 1997. *Local economy*. Cambridge, MA: MIT Press.

Collins, Chris and Phil Branigan. 1997. Quotative inversion. *Natural Language and Linguistic Theory* 15:1–41.

Dikken, Marcel den. 2006. *Relators and linkers: The syntax of predication, predicate inversion, and copulas*. Cambridge, MA: MIT Press.

Emonds, Joseph. 1970. *Root and structure-preserving transformations*. Doctoral dissertation, MIT, Cambridge, MA.

Gallego, Ángel and Juan Uriagereka. 2006. Sub-extraction from subjects. Paper presented at West Coast Conference on Formal Linguistics (WCCFL) 25 and Linguistic Symposium on Romance Languages (LSRL) 36, 1 April.

Grimshaw, Jane. 1997. Projection, heads and optimality. *Linguistic Inquiry* 28:373–422.

Haegeman, Liliane. 1994. *Introduction to government and binding theory*, 2nd edition. Oxford: Blackwell Publishing.

Haegeman, Liliane. 2005. *Thinking Syntactically*. Oxford: Wiley-Blackwell.

Hale, Ken and Samuel Jay Keyser. 1993. On argument structure and the lexical expression of syntactic relations. In *The view from Building 20*, eds. by Ken Hale and Samuel Jay Keyser, 53–109. Cambridge, MA: MIT Press.

Hale, Ken and Samuel Jay Keyser. 2002. *Prolegomenon to a theory of argument structure*. Cambridge, MA: MIT Press.

Huddleston, Rodney and Geoffrey K. Pullum. 2005. *A student's introduction to English grammar*. Cambridge: Cambridge University Press.

Koopman, Hilda and Dominique Sportiche. 1991. The position of subjects. *Lingua* 85:211–258.

Matos, Gabriela. 2013. Quotative inversion in Peninsular Portuguese and Spanish, and in English. *Catalan Journal of Linguistics* 12:111–130.

Sasaki, Shigetsugu. 2010. *Indonesiago no nakaniwa: Bunpoohen* (A courtyard of Indonesian: Grammar part). Privately printed and accessible at http://homepage3.nifty.com/sanggar/mag/magframe.htm.

Sneddon, James Neil. 2010. *Indonesian: A comprehensive grammar*, 2nd edition. London and New York: Routledge.

Suñer, Margarita. 2000. The syntax of direct quotes with special reference to Spanish and English. *Natural Language and Linguistic Theory* 18:525–557.

Williams, Edwin. 1980. Predication. *Linguistic Inquiry* 11:203–238.

Phase Theory and Its Consequences:
The Initial and Recursive Symbol *S*

編　者　　安井美代子・水口　学

発行者　　武村哲司

2016 年 7 月 21 日　第 1 版第 1 刷発行©

発行所　　株式会社　開 拓 社
〒113-0023　東京都文京区向丘 1-5-2
電話　(03) 5842-8900（代表）
振替　00160-8-39587
http://www.kaitakusha.co.jp

印刷　株式会社　あるむ

ISBN978-4-7589-2228-9　C3080